THANKS FOR THE MEMORY

THANKS FOR THE MEMORY

□

A personal spotlight on
special people in entertainment

HUBERT GREGG

LONDON
VICTOR GOLLANCZ LTD
1983

© Hubert Gregg, 1983

British Library Cataloguing in Publication Data
Gregg, Hubert
  Thanks for the memory: a personal spotlight on
  special people in entertainment.
  1. Amusements—Biography
  I. Title
  791'.092'4   GV1203

  ISBN 0-575-03335-5

Designed by Roger Lightfoot
Typeset by Tradespools Ltd, Frome, Somerset
Printed in Great Britain by the Camelot Press, Southampton

FOR CARMEL, KATE AND ROBERT HUBERT
WHO BEGAN *MY* LIFE

CONTENTS

LIST OF ILLUSTRATIONS

AUTHOR'S NOTE

In the late seventies, I began writing and presenting a series of broadcasts for B.B.C. Radio Two in which I turned, we said, 'a personal spotlight on special people in entertainment'. I chose for a title 'A Touch of Genius'. After two years of preparation we were about to go on the air when the Controller discovered that another had nipped in with a show of his own using my title. Reluctantly, I changed to 'I Call It Genius'. A touch didactic I thought, but no matter.

A series of eight one-hour programmes was followed by a second series of eight. Continuing into the eighties, I presented a similar series which I named 'I Call It Style'—and a second of these. Throughout, there had been kind inquiries from listeners about the availability of the stories in book form and when, in 1982, the B.B.C. began to repeat both series the letters came in again. I thought the idea might work but it was a chance meeting with my old friend Jimmy Leasor that provided impetus. Leasor—who created the remarkable Jason Love and his obsession with Cord motor cars—is supercharged himself. He whisked me straight round to Henrietta Street and introduced me to David Burnett and wheels were set, at once, in motion.

I have divided the stories into two sections—'Genius' and 'Style'—and given to each its individual title. The overall title of the book is taken from a nostalgic series which I have presented weekly since 1971.

ACKNOWLEDGEMENTS

My thanks, not only to those who lived the lives, but to:

Messrs. Chappell and Company for permission to print selections from lyrics by writers whose works they publish—sometimes through subsidiary channels.

E.M.I. Music for like kind permission.

(for details of the above I refer you to the following page.)

Phyllis Robinson, producer of my B.B.C. series that bears the same title as this book, for diligent delving into archives and serendipitous findings.

Carmel, my wife, for untiring help and patient encouragement....

and James Leasor who must take the final responsibility, since without his enthusiasm and egging-on the words might not have been printed.

The sources of information gleaned over a lifetime are mighty difficult to define. Especially for one with a retentive memory and the joyous experience of more than fifty years of association with theatre people and film people, whether they be actors, composers, word writers, producers, directors or carriers of whatever kind of can. With regard to the subjects in this volume, I have adored their works, I have seen and heard them play and sing, sung their songs ... watched them dance ... in some cases, talked and imbibed with them into small hours made great by conversation. I have read much that has been said about them Over the years, everything they have said about themselves and one another. When it came to a matter of a date or a place of birth, the success or failure of a show—all too often judged by the bald statistic of the number of performances, I have had natural recourse to a book of reference. I have verified by reference to a second and third reference. I have juggled with misinformation, going back and back again to personal memory which is often enough, thank God, gloriously devoid of misprint.

To any who, at any time, may have written words about the subjects herein remembered ... to friends – theirs and mine – who have reminisced ... very particularly, to the voices preserved in the archives of the B.B.C. and the preservers, my gratitude. But, more than all, to the subjects themselves my thanks for so many memories.

LYRICAL ACKNOWLEDGEMENTS

'Dames' © 1934 Remick Music Corp., sub-published B. Feldman & Co.

'I'm young and healthy' © 1932 Whitmark & Son, sub-published B. Feldman & Co.

'Let's do it' © 1928 Harms Inc.

'Love for sale' © 1930 Harms Inc.

'You're the top' © 1934 Harms Inc.

'At long last, love' © 1938 Chappell & Co. Inc.

'Ace in the hole' © 1941 Chappell & Co. Inc.

'Most gentlemen don't like love' © 1938 Chappell & Co. Inc.

'But in the morning, no!' © 1939 Chappell & Co. Inc.

'Make it another old-fashioned, please' © 1940 Chappell & Co. Inc.

'Ev'ry time we say goodbye' © 1944 Chappell & Co. Inc.

'Brush up your Shakespeare' © 1949 Cole Porter

'I am loved' © 1950 Cole Porter

'I get a kick out of you' © 1934 Harms Inc.

'Down in the depths on the 90th floor' © 1936 Chappell & Co. Inc.

'Thank you so much, Mrs Louseboro'-Goodby' © 1934 Harms Inc.

'Don't fence me in' © 1934 Harms Inc.

'Funny face' © 1927 New World Music Corp.

'I'm building up to an awful let-down' © 1935 Bourne Inc.

'On your toes' © 1936 Chappell & Co. Inc.

'Any old place with you' © 1919 Jerome H. Remick & Co.

'Mountain greenery' © 1926 Harms Inc.

'You are too beautiful' © 1932 Rodart Music Corp.

'There's a small hotel' © 1936 Chappell & Co. Inc.

'I wish I were in love again' © 1937 Chappell & Co. Inc.

'I like to recognise the tune' © 1939 Chappell & Co. Inc.

'Bewitched' © 1941 Chappell & Co. Inc.

'To keep my love alive' © 1944 Harms Inc.

'Spring is here' © 1938 The Big Three Music/CBS Songs Ltd.

'Poor little rich girl' © 1925 Ascherberg, Hopwood & Crew Ltd.

'Hello, young lovers' © 1951 Richard Rodgers & Oscar Hammerstein 2nd.

'There's a rainbow round my shoulder © 1928 Bourne & Co., sub-published Francis, Day & Hunter Ltd.

'Why is there ever goodbye?' © 1930 Chappell & Co. Inc.

'Sweet so-and-so' © 1931 Harms Inc.

BUSBY BERKELEY
Dames

Buzz in 1932, surrounded by some early Berkeley girls. They
appeared in his third Eddie Cantor subject *The Kid from Spain*.

BUSBY BERKELEY

In Britain where we have nightingales singing for some in London—Busby Berkeley would have heard them, there's no question, he'd have signed them up—we say 'Barkley'. In America they say 'Berkeley' (as written). So . . . to Buzz, as they called him for short, we raise our derbies—or Darbies—or any other kind of hat we may be wearing.

WHAT DO YOU GO FOR,
GO SEE A SHOW FOR,
TELL THE TRUTH YOU GO
TO SEE THOSE BEAUTIFUL DAMES . . .

So sang Dick Powell, using words written by Al Dubin. Busby Berkeley loved beautiful dames. He married six, not because he'd rather have six than a mere one, but because they just tended not to stay the course. A compulsive proposer he may have been, but he understood the need. He gave dames to us, for the first time ever in glorious close-up, gift wrapped, at a time when men adored girls and girls adored being adored.

Busby Berkeley . . . dance director extraordinary, designer of movement—even of clothes, certainly of bathing suits; maker of unforgettable movies like *42nd Street, Gold Diggers of 1933, '35, '37, Dames, Footlight Parade*, and many, many more. But those early ones left an indelible mark, especially on me, a schoolboy. Buzz did me a special service in focusing my attention on the Berkeley Girls. They were an enchanting group of females, with an average age of about twenty—not as young as I was but something to make growing up worth while.

The word 'Genius' has been variously defined. According to the Oxford Dictionary it is 'an extraordinary capacity for imaginative creation, original thought, invention or discovery'. That fits in Berkeley's case. Carlyle defined it as 'a transcendent capacity of taking trouble', which also fits. Samuel Butler comments: 'It might more fitly be described as a supreme capacity for getting its possessors into trouble of all kinds and keeping them therein so long as the genius remains.' In our own time John Osborne has used an adjective, 'unrepeatable'. There certainly will never be another Buzz Berkeley. The circumstances in which he came to spectacular notice can never be repeated. The innocence of the age in which he shone for us and we basked will, like youth, never come again.

I'M YOUNG AND HEALTHY, sang Dick Powell in another film,
    using Al Dubin's words again,
SO LET'S BE BOLD!
IN A YEAR OR TWO OR THREE
MAYBE WE WILL BE TOO OLD . . .

In fact, it could be said that Berkeley's cinematic heyday spanned just such a period—four, maybe five years. He went on making films for a quarter of a century, but when you blaze a trail you don't continue to go it alone. While I enjoyed *Babes in Arms* in 1939—the musical numbers were marvellous even without patterns and top shots—I didn't remember that Busby Berkeley had anything to do with it. I shall never forget that he created the 'stage show' *Pretty Lady* in *42nd Street*.

According to Joan Blondell, one of the Berkeley stars and also Mrs Dick Powell, Buzz knew nothing about dancing or dance steps. 'He made the camera dance', she said. Miss Blondell didn't know a lot about dancing, though she came from Vaudeville. Choreographer Hermes Pan, on the other hand, knew quite a bit:

His geometrical designs and his top shots and his idea of opening up a little stage and making it grow into a huge football field ... It was complete fantasy but it captured the imagination. It was something that people had never seen before. He was quite an innovator. Of course he didn't rely on dancing. His medium was the camera, not dance.

Hal Wallis, who produced *Gold Diggers of 1933*, was more specific:

He had a mathematical mind. Ordinarily a choreographer will lay out a number and then put the cameras around and pick up shots here and there. Buzz had his numbers cut in his own mind. He shot with one camera and when he finished shooting it was only a matter really of splicing the film together because it was shot with such precision and everything he did fitted into the pattern. He was really a genius.

Busby Berkeley was born in 1895. In that year William Enos was running a repertory company and acting too, to save a salary. His wife, Gertrude Berkeley, acted because it came naturally. She took a little time off in the late autumn and on November 29th she gave birth to a boy. Like the girl in the film you could say he was born in a trunk, but you wouldn't have had to let mother hear you. I've never been quite sure what it is that makes stage folk want something better for their offspring. Is it the uncertainty of the business? Are they ashamed of their calling? Or is it professional jealousy? There was an older son, George, who had graduated from Military Academy but had drifted on to the boards. Mother was going to try again.

Two other members of the company were honoured when first names were under discussion: Amy Busby and William Gillette. So we had a babe in arms called Busby Berkeley William Enos. It may be significant that, later, he chose to take his mother's name—though it was also alliterative and looked better on the bills.

His mother forbade him to enter the theatre except at

matinées. This concession proved her undoing. Buzz got himself
into the wings when his brother George was on the stage in the
play *Under Two Flags*. George was wearing flowing robes and
trying to play an Arab. It couldn't have been much of a part
because during the action he was able to sidle over to the wings,
wrap young Buzz in his cloak and re-enter with a small aspirant
clinging to one leg.

Gertrude Berkeley—and father too, we suppose, though
mother seems always to have been a prime mover—did send Buzz
to Military Academy. Here, presumably, he picked up a little
mathematics; certainly he admits to hanging alarm clocks down
air vents, timed to go off in the middle of the night. In 1914 he
graduated and went into a shoe factory, doing well for three years
among the shoes. Later he was to do very well indeed with the
soles of shoes in his staggering 'Lullaby of Broadway' presenta-
tion that was the high spot of *Gold Diggers of 1935*.

But first came the War. It was in April of 1917 that America
entered and Busby Berkeley enlisted. He got bored with re-
training and having boasted that he could play the bugle found
himself appointed company bugler. One night he forgot about
'Taps', the American version of 'Lights Out', and got into a
pillow fight in the hut. Suddenly he recalled his bugling duty, but
before he could dress they bundled him out as he was and
slammed the door. He blew taps stark naked, which, the duty
officer thought, showed insufficient respect for whatever it is
you're supposed to show respect for in the Army. But he got his
commission and plumped for the artillery because he'd heard
they would be first overseas.

The crossing gave Buzz his first taste of active service food.
With typical flair, he slipped the purser a few dollars, and he and
a friend lived high off the Army hog—on bread and cheese, but it
was Camembert, and it was accompanied by champagne (the boat
must have been making a return trip). Immediately on landing,
Buzz and his champagne buddy went A.W.O.L. because they
wanted to have a look at the Bordeaux red light district. With
military police swarming around they got a couple of local ladies

to lend them some gear. Clad as tarts, they toured the town unmolested—at least by police. When the military police closed in, two pukkah tarts hid them in a basket until the all-clear. After two memorable days, they sneaked back into camp—as males. Nobody guessed they had been away.

Buzz Berkeley was one of 92 out of 2000 artillery men to be ordered for special training at Saumur. One day a prophetic parade happened. It was one of Berkeley's military chores to take company drill which, as I know from experience, is one of the aspects of military life that appealed to actors.(It was the only aspect of military life that appealed to me.) The actor—and future director—in Buzz came to the fore. It wasn't enough for him to shout words of command. With the Colonel's permission to try something new, he worked out a trick drill, numbered the movements, gave the section leaders instructions and began the parade. The Colonel was astonished to witness the result: 1,200 men marching, counter-marching, performing every move in the drill book in total silence.

Buzz's older brother, George, persisted with acting. Not finding the success he'd hoped for, he took to drugs and one day was found dead on a park bench. Understandably, when Buzz came back from the War his mother, Gertrude Berkeley, did everything she knew to keep him out of what we call—with unintentional *double entendre*—'the business'. But he went into it. For him there could be no other choice. Gertrude resigned herself to his decision, travelling with him as his critic, and perhaps also as a frightener off of potential marriage partners.

In the early twenties we may note that Busby Berkeley is stage managing and acting in revue and producing and directing for women's clubs. To drum up a little business he hangs upside down from the wing of an aeroplane in flight, dropping balloons with tickets attached. Making those later top shots at Warners and wandering around on girders in the studio roof to plan them must have seemed tame by comparison.

Berkeley's biggest acting stint happened in 1923 in a revival of *Irene*. For three years he played the effeminate fashion fellow known as 'Madame Lucy'. Directing was what he wanted to do but in those days acting paid more, though of course if you could land both jobs at once that was better still. Any spare cash Buzz handed to his mother, who began investing in antiques.

At one time Buzz was directing plays in stock, and the boss said, 'We're putting on a musical.' 'I can't do that,' said Buzz, 'I don't know anything about directing musicals—what about the dancing?' 'We'll get a girl in,' they said. Next time Buzz said, 'What do you want a girl in for, I can do it!' Broadway beckoned with a show called *Holka Polka*, but it said a quick goodbye. In 1927 it beckoned again, and this time Buzz would be on the Great White Way to stay.

It was Lew Fields who employed Buzz, and the new show was an adaptation of Mark Twain's *A Connecticut Yankee in King Arthur's Court*. Herb Fields, son of Lew, who wrote the book, called it, more simply, *A Connecticut Yankee*. It had music and lyrics by Richard Rodgers and Lorenz Hart. Berkeley had, by now, something of a reputation as a choreographer—yet he'd never had a dancing lesson. Nothing in the entertainment business succeeds like bluff. In one scene in *A Connecticut Yankee*, Queen Guinevere holds a dancing class. Berkeley thought he'd begin with the Queen showing her ladies the five positions of dance, the only trouble being that he didn't even know the first position. So he wandered round at rehearsal with his hand on his brow looking creatively thoughtful. Suddenly, he said to one of the girls: 'I think I'll start off by having the Queen show you the first position ...' The girl said: 'Like this?' Buzz took a sly look and said, 'Yes ... yes, that's it.' Then he said to another girl: 'The second position ...' And she got into the second position, and so forth. Thus choreographer Busby Berkeley learned the five positions of dance.

A Connecticut Yankee opened. The press announced: 'A new dance director has been born on Broadway.' It ran for more than four hundred performances. Rodgers and Hart, not surprisingly, seemed pleased, and now asked Buzz to direct *Present Arms*. Although not as successful as *A Connecticut Yankee*, the show gave Buzz two contracts. He took over the comedy lead before the opening. One of the songs he had to sing was 'You took advantage of me'. On the opening night he nearly caused Lorenz Hart to have a seizure. Hart was standing in the wings, when, after one chorus, Berkeley's mind suddenly went blank. Some actors say nothing on these occasions; others ad lib. To ad lib a Larry Hart lyric is quite a feat. In later years, Larry and Buzz were able to smile but, as we say, 'on the night' the great Mr Hart had to beat his breast and listen as Buzz came out with:

WHEN I WAS WALKING DOWN THE STREET,
I SAW A LITTLE BIRD WHO CALLED 'TWEET TWEET' . . .
I SHOOK MY HEAD AND SAID INSTEAD . . .
'COS YOU TOOK ADVANTAGE OF ME . . .

It was following the opening of *Present Arms* that the *New York Times* wrote about the Berkeley technique on stage. Later it would move to celluloid and the same instincts, the same touch of genius—with one exceptional factor—would come into play. For now, the *Times* said:

Busby Berkeley assumes the mantle of a kind of modern prophet, though he himself probably hasn't found it out yet. What Berkeley did in *A Connecticut Yankee* and, even to a greater extent, in *Present Arms*, was to discover a new and sound basis on which to build for novelty. If there can be such a thing as high brow jazz dancing, his creations cannot escape being so catalogued. He creates none of these dances in advance. In fact his inspiration seems to come from having the girls in front of him on the stage, ready for work.

This was the exceptional factor. In the cinema Buzz took very much to planning in advance—perhaps a consciousness of the cost of keeping a studio idle while you think had something to do with it.

Buzz left the cast of *Present Arms* to direct the dance sequences for yet another hit show, *The Earl Carroll Vanities of 1928*. By now he was pretty steadily in demand—usually for doctoring shows, bringing something special to them. His first Broadway show as director-in-chief was *A Night in Venice*, again a hit. He had been sharing an apartment with his mother. Now, at her suggestion, he bought an estate in Dover, New Hampshire with a 24-room house and moved her in with her ever-growing collection of antiques.

While Buzz was in Philadelphia with *A Night in Venice* he met an actress named Esther Muir and they began going out together. When he had to travel to London for the Shubert Brothers Buzz took her with him. He also took his mother. As Esther travelled back on one ship and the Berkeleys on another, somebody must have said something to somebody. Back in New York Esther insisted on a date being settled for the wedding. While Buzz was on a try-out for the Shuberts in Baltimore, J. J. Shubert caught him making a dash from the theatre and asked him where he was going. 'To City Hall to buy a marriage licence,' shouted Buzz. 'Fool!' Shubert shouted back, but to no avail: Buzz and his first wife were married in the theatre and J. J. threw a party on the stage.

Shubert asked Buzz to produce the French farce *The Street Singer*. Buzz not only produced it, he also directed and choreographed it and became the first in the American theatre ever to do so, paving the way for Jerome Robbins, Michael Kidd and Gower Champion many years later. The press said: 'The dances Busby Berkeley arranged for *The Street Singer* were so numerous, intricate, exciting and well done that nothing else in the show mattered . . .' Of the Berkeley girls, they said: 'They are about the fastest-stepping throng of pretty girls ever to enliven a stage. His tireless, peppy, pulchritudinous chorus won salvos of applause.' Berkeley himself won more applause for the *9.15 Revue*. It contained Harold Arlen's first song 'Get happy'.

When he got to Hollywood Buzz was forever pushing his camera higher. He confessed that he left his mark on at least five of the Warner sound stages by cutting holes in the roof. He must have gone through the theatre roof when he heard the score for his next stage effort. Lew Leslie, the famous producer of the *Blackbirds* shows, asked him to direct his *International Revue*. Nothing, surely, could delight a director of musicals more than to have standards in the score, though, of course, nobody knows they are going to be standards. Standards are funny things: no composer can sit down to write one, they tend to happen. Dorothy Fields and Jimmy McHugh created the songs, and two of them, 'Exactly like you' and 'On the sunny side of the street', would last for ever. Lew Leslie's *International Review* was filled with talent, some of it barely beginning to flower: Gertrude Lawrence was the star but in the orchestra pit were Benny Goodman, Harry James and Tommy Dorsey.

'Whoopee' was a popular word of the day—it was a popular pastime. It was also the title of a Broadway hit in 1926 and Hollywood bought a neat package. Buzz didn't think much of film musicals at that time, for it seemed to him that hit shows were being hurried to the coast from Broadway and whipped on to celluloid with little regard for the new medium. He discouraged the William Morris Agency from arranging for him to follow Horace Greeley's advice: 'Go West, young man.' Finally, under pressure, he said: 'With a great star, a great producer and a great property I might consider it'. 'Eddie Cantor?' they said. 'Mm,' he said. 'Flo Ziegfeld *and* Goldwyn?' 'Yes ...' 'You want a property? How about *Whoopee?*'

Thornton Freeland directed *Whoopee* and Buzz staged the dances. Normally the director controls the shooting of the dance sequences too, but Buzz got Sam Goldwyn to agree that he should film his own work. Not only did he stagger the studio with his first-ever overhead shots (to say nothing of the girls underneath this cinematic sword of Damocles), he scored another first by putting the prettiest of the girls into close-up. Goldwyn caught him at it and asked him what he thought he was doing—close ups of chorus girls? 'Why not?' said Buzz. 'We're paying these beautiful girls, let the public get a good look at them.' Goldwyn, to whom the idea of a beautiful money's worth was irresistible, had no hesitation in agreeing.

Buzz and the camera—he never used more than one—were soon firm friends. He became wedded to it; and unwedded to his wife. Mr Berkeley and Mrs Berkeley the first were, it seems, incompatible, something that one couldn't say about Buzz and his new found love. Six musicals followed in two years, including two more with Eddie Cantor, *Palmy Days* and *The Kid from Spain*. Buzz was proving himself to be a good judge of feminine talent; his Berkeley girls included Paulette Goddard, Lucille Ball (Goldwyn didn't think much of her but Buzz got her on the payroll), two Virginias—Grey and Bruce—Carole Landis, Jeanne Craine and Betty Grable.

Over this period Busby Berkeley did well for the movie moguls, but their distrust of the cinema's musical future had become deeply rooted before his arrival in Hollywood. It was Daryll Zanuck of Warners who stopped Buzz from making a retreat to Broadway. He was 'going to have one more go at a musical', he said, and invited Berkeley to stage the numbers. *42nd Street* was, one might say, the film that saved Hollywood musicals. It pulled Warner Brothers out of the red but, more importantly, it made 35mm history, initiating half a decade of musical cinema that will never be equalled. Warren and Dubin wrote the score and gave Buzz four smash hits to work on, four standards in one movie.

42nd Street, for me, was the beginning of Busby Berkeley. I had seen *Whoopee* and *Palmy Days* and *The Kid from Spain* when I was at school, but it was *42nd Street* that really captured my adolescent imagination. This backstage story to begin and end them all was directed by Lloyd Bacon with such pace that when Berkeley takes over the join is undetectable. Warner Baxter plays the ailing Julian Marsh who is to direct Jones and Barry's new musical *Pretty Lady*. How much will it cost to put it on? £14,000. Today it would eat up a quarter of a million, but yesterday was a time when only the talent was priceless. The story has everything—ambition, jostling for the front line, failure turning into success, Cinderella to go or not to go to the ball. It's true enough to life, but Hollywood sugars the pill, dresses it all up and dishes it out in one hour thirty minutes while you sit and suck your Sno-frute.

Berkeley's contribution is sheer genius. In shooting the earlier numbers he plays fair, giving you nothing that wouldn't be possible on a theatre stage until 'I'm young and healthy'. Here Buzz suddenly takes his one camera away up into what we call the 'flies', the ceiling of the stage. Beyond them, up through the roof, we are privileged to look down on the patterning Berkeley girls and see them as the audience never could. Then, down comes the camera again to a real angle: a tantalizing mixture of stage and cinema—to prepare us, perhaps? It's as though Berkeley is toying with us, trying out our willingness to accept a brand new technique. Ruby Keeler begins singing '42nd street', and we sense that Buzz has a surprise in store. She opens solo. This one girl in black shorts and black tights that don't quite meet is the teasing, simple appearance of the bud of the number before it bursts into bloom.

Now for the surprise. Buzz pulls back his camera and we see that Miss Keeler is dancing, not on a black stage as we thought, but on the roof of a taxi. She clambers down and we are in 42nd Street with more people milling around than a stage—and certainly Jones and Barry's budget—could begin to think of carrying. The theatre is gone now and we are in the Busby Berkeley world of no walls and no limits. As he builds to the crescendo, the Berkeley girls, stockings and suspenders ('garters' to them) peeping through the slit skirts, dance and dance. What's this huge construction work we see—is it the elevated railway King Kong will make a grab at in a year or two's time? Taxis galore. Now the girls are gone ... no, here they come again, moving sideways, backs to the camera, each carrying a tall piece of scenery. Up the steps they go, still keeping their backs to us, climbing, climbing.

All at once, the girls turn to us and we see Berkeley's miracle brain-child. Each girl has disappeared behind the piece of scenery she is carrying and they make a pattern of skyscrapers,

The Berkeley girls and a few boys in the 'no walls, no limits'
sequence from my favourite Berkeley film – *42nd Street*.

rising into the distance. Julian Marsh, the Director, looking on
the verge of collapse (though we know he is going to make it), sits
on a stairway and lights one more, clearly forbidden, cigarette.
Up comes the closing music and the titles tell us the Berkeley
dream is all over.

Like the pushed back walls of Jones and Barry's theatre, Busby
Berkeley's career now opened up. Berkeley had a one-film
contract but before *42nd Street* was completed Zanuck had signed
him up for seven years. The *New York Herald Express* was to
confirm his judgement: '*42nd Street* is a cinematic effort by which
Busby Berkeley, and he alone, is responsible for the current
return of celluloid musicals. The beauty and originality of his
dances top everything yet shown on the screen . . .'

Buzz was already at work on his next film. 'Warner Brothers,'
screamed the poster, 'surpass the glories of *42nd Street* with *Gold
Diggers of 1933*. Bigger stars, more gorgeous girls, more lavish
spectacles.' It added: 'Of course you'll see it.' We did, and loved
it. Ginger Rogers led the opening song, 'We're in the money',
dressed in nothing but dollars. Warren and Dubin wrote the
song, trying to tell anyone who'd listen that the depression was
over. The story gave the lie to them because before the girls get
halfway through the number the Sheriff's men arrive to close the
show. But the mood throughout is optimism. In those days
nobody whined, everybody hoped . . . and sweated.

In these films, it seemed, the girls never stopped. Buzz used
them like toys—he had to. He explained to them what he was
going to do, using a blackboard, and he picked himself a nucleus
of sixteen. (The section leaders of his parade ground drills?) They
would be the lynch-pins of his apparently hare-brained top shots
(and, more often, bottom shots), which were invariably beautiful
and pre-eminently tasteful. They didn't know how it would all
look on film, being happy to leave it to Buzz with his one
camera.

In *Gold Diggers of 1933* occurred the famous waltz with the girls
playing, or pretending to play, neon-framed violins. Top shots in

A top-shot in the dark. The neon violin sequence from *Gold Diggers of 1933* – Ruby Keeler, centre, amid a ring of wired up Berkeley girls.

the dark, with only the violin shapes visible. Each girl was wired
to a battery, and the violins were seen first to dance, then to move
about to make up one huge violin. Watching the smooth result
you would never know that they were having an earthquake in
California at the time. The Press were wildly enthusiastic. The
Los Angeles Record called *Gold Diggers* '...a dazzling, eye-
paralysing, ear tickling creation that makes all the other musical
films look like Delancy Street peep-shows. The star of the picture
is the gentle man who does not appear in it. Busby Berkeley, the
geometrically-minded lad who created the dance sequences, has
done a perfectly amazing job ...' (It is to be wondered what
director Mervyn Le Roy thought about that.)

Out of the studio Buzz found the time to marry his second
wife. In it he was dreaming up his most ambitious production
number to date—a waterfall song. The movie was *Footlight
Parade*, starring Jimmy Cagney and, for the third time, Ruby
Keeler. Ruby Keeler didn't swim too well, but Buzz had it all
worked out. 'We're going to have you all do porpoise dives,' he
said. 'It's a glass-sided tank, you see. We shoot you under the
water. As you swim up towards the camera, give me a nice smile.'
Keeler was petrified. 'Of course you can,' said Buzz before she
had time to say she couldn't. 'Just splash around and practise a
bit ... You'll do it.' She did. It was gruelling work for the girls
who swam a six-day week and a fifteen-hour day, but not one
complained. So exciting did the girls find working for Buzz that a
Berkeley Girl Association was begun and continued for many
years in Los Angeles.

His third big musical stint in 1933 was to stage the numbers for
Roman Scandals. The new movie starred Eddie Cantor, with a
banquet of beautiful girls in support.

Warner Brothers and Berkeley, their blue-eyed boy, began
1934 with a movie called *Wonder Bar* after the stage success ...
very much after. The essential thing about being a blue-eyed boy
is that your eyes continue to sparkle; you are only as good as your
last breathtaking creation. Buzz was constantly under pressure to
take away the breath, not only of his producers but of the critics

and the public who had come to expect so much and would go on expecting more. In *Wonder Bar* they were not disappointed. When he created 'Don't say goodnight', Buzz decided to surround his cameras with mirrors. 'You can't,' said lighting cameraman Sol Polito, 'you'll photograph the camera . . . and us!' Buzz sat in his office, stood a pencil on his desk and, around it, positioned eight powder compacts borrowed from the girls. The idea was soon born and growing. He had the studio build him an octagon of mirrors thirty feet high. Somewhere within them he placed his camera but by a mixture of Berkeley mathematics and magic as it was never seen by us. The effect was indeed breathtaking: a dozen or so girls and boys moving, dancing—apparently in their hundreds—into infinity.

In his next movie, *Fashions of 1934*, Buzz was up to more tricks. Sammy Fain and Irving Kahal, who had written *By a Waterfall*, wrote the songs. For 'Spin a little web of dreams' Buzz had his girls dressed in ostrich feathers as galley slaves rowing a huge ostrich feather boat with ostrich feather oars—clearly, the water couldn't resist. High above, on ostrich feathers, sat Venus. We also had a spider's web of girls shot from above, and a Hall of Human Harps—white-clad nun-like females playing huge harps. The front of each harp, the straight bit, was a captive girl looking like a decoration on a cake, with small ostrich feathers round her top—and round her bottom, and a satin gift ribbon round her middle. One outraged mother wrote to a newspaper protesting: 'I don't want my daughter growing up to be a human harp.' The girls made no complaints, nor did we watching males.

It wasn't all fun and girls for Busby Berkeley. 'There was fun,' he said, 'and certainly there was excitement, but what I remember mostly is stress and strain and exhaustion. I worried about being able to come up with new ideas and then I worried about how they'd go over with the public.' Berkeley's night and day devotion to his work played matrimonial havoc. His second marriage ended on the cutting room floor. Jealous associates dubbed him 'the million dollar director'. This was roughly the cost of the legal tug-of-war over his services engaged in by

Goldwyn and Warners. The critics continued to rave: 'He is an optometrist extraordinary,' said one; 'A kaleidoscopic genius,' said another. Edison, an early dabbler in movies, defines 'genius' as 'one per cent inspiration and ninty-nine per cent perspiration'.

In 1934 Berkeley created the numbers for *Dames*, one of his best pictures; three pairs of writers worked on the score. '14 NOTED STARS' said the posters, mentioning six, 'AND HUNDREDS OF GLORIOUS BUSBY BERKELEY BEAUTIES ...' I remember in particular his direction of the song Warren and Dubin wrote for Dick Powell to sing to Ruby Keeler, 'I only have eyes for you'. Buzz took us out into the New York streets, on the subway, even on to the Staten Island Ferry. The poor Berkeley girls were sorely tried; each had to wear a mask with Ruby Keeler's face painted on it, and looked more like Ruby Keeler than Ruby herself. They must have hated it. Ruby Keeler was pretty, but if you're a girl and have a pretty face you wouldn't, surely, want to have to wear somebody else's.

Dames had a wonderful title number, in which Buzz pulled every camera trick in the book—his book, he wrote it. The girls, in white tops and hats and black up-to-the-waist tights, made their famous patterns with Buzz shooting down from the roof. When he wants to get a closer look the girls shoot up at us one after another from floor to camera into beautiful close-up. Tricky for focussing, said Sol Polito, but Buzz was ahead of him. He had each girl taken up on a wire and perfectly focused, then as the camera turned she was swung sixty feet down to the floor, into the arms of her co-Berkeley beauties. Then he had the film printed in reverse. The effect was unbelievable. My memory of movies is that a girl will do a lot for a close-up, but these must have been terrified out of their tights. On screen, however, they look as cool as a Knickerbocker Glory. *Dames* was another Berkeley hit; after seeing it one critic coined a new word: 'cinematerpsichorean'.

Now came Berkeley's first screen chance as director-in-chief.

The film was, is and will always be a classic—*Gold Diggers of 1935*. 'Give Berkeley anything he wants', Zanuck had said two years earlier. He now asked for fifty-six white grand pianos. They were only the shells of pianos but they would have fooled anybody, and while I don't think the Berkeley girls would have convinced us they were playing them this hardly mattered. The pianos danced in waltz tempo, though we didn't know how. If you do know and look closely you can see little pairs of black-clad legs, clearly belonging to fifty-six small humans who waltz the pianos round from underneath, following marks on the floor. The first time you see the picture you won't spot them in a thousand frames; Buzz knew the quickness of the camera—or the legs—would deceive the eye. Never were our optics more delightfully deluded.

For *Gold Diggers of '35*, Dubin and Warren had written a jewel of a song called 'Lullaby of Broadway'. Buzz had no idea how to begin it, and while he was deliberating Al Jolson walked into his office and said, 'I've heard this song ... Dubin and Warren are doing the numbers for my picture *Go into your Dance*. How about my using this?' Buzz said, 'To tell you the truth, Al, I can't think of a way to stage it. Give me until tomorrow. If I don't come up with an idea you can have it.' History took a firm hand and Buzz had an overnight brainwave. He had invented a monorail so that his single camera could travel, with Buzz and Sol Polito as passengers ... up, down, around at will. He began the number with a black screen. In the distance a tiny white dot, Wini Shaw's face. As she sings he moves in on her at a barely perceptible pace, taking a whole verse and chorus, until, finally, she is in huge close-up. Then he swings above her looking down on her face, which dissolves into a top shot of Manhattan. Despite that 'We never see a headline 'bout a breadline' song from the '33 *Gold Diggers*, there was widespread unemployment among actors and dancers in Hollywood. Buzz decided to do his cinematic bit towards making it a shortening breadline. For 'Lullaby of Broadway' he said, 'Get me a hundred dancers.' The Berkeley girls, being in constant work, are as chubby as could be, but one of the joys—and sadnesses—of seeing this sequence is the eager look on the lean faces of the men, dancing as though their lives depend upon it. Certainly their next meals did. Dubin and Warren won an Oscar for 'Lullaby of Broadway'. It was undeniably a superb song but Buzz had given it a treatment for which any writer should go down on his knees.

These were the halcyon years of Busby Berkeley. According to Hazlitt, 'The world has a standing pique against genius.' No doubt Berkeley's huge success planted envy in a few of the meaner professional minds. Did some kind soul slip him a Mickey at a certain party in Pacific Pallisades? While he was driving back along the tricky Pacific coast highway a tyre blew on his car and threw him into headlong collision. Three people died and Buzz was on trial for manslaughter. Twice the jury failed to agree. At a third trial he was acquitted, but by this time work and worry, to say nothing of legal costs, had all but undermined him. One of the penalties of success, especially in the golden Hollywood round, is that you get charged a hundred times more than the ordinary man on the Boulevard. The fees ran to $100,000, in today's money something like a quarter of a million pounds.

There are two kinds of people who make public entertainment: the creators and the money men. The two rarely see eye to eye. In films these money men are known as 'the front office', and the Warner Brothers front office now began to lean on Buzz over costs. At one point in filming *Stars over Broadway* he got so fed up with the cheese-paring that he said he'd shoot one number without a set at all, merely with a black stage. It was a complete success. Unfortunately this only confirmed to the money men that Buzz didn't need money.

The depression had been perfect ground for Berkeley's escapist blooms. Was the public taste now changing? Such assessments are for the money boys to guess at and their guess, all too often, isn't as good as yours. The last spectacular throw for Warners and for Buzz was *Hollywood Hotel*. The shaken state of the front office faith is evident from the billing: Dick Powell,

Rosemary Lane, Frances Langford and Hugh Herbert headed the cast. Warners even contracted the popular Benny Goodman band for insurance plus the film gossip writer Louella Parsons who drove Buzz up the studio wall because she would look into the camera lens.

The 1938 *Gold Diggers in Paris* was economy gone mad. Buzz did his best, but even he couldn't surmount the threadbareness of the production. He must have got a new lease of spirit when, in 1939, he moved to MGM. Judy Garland starred for him in *Babes in Arms*, *Strike up the Band*, *Babes on Broadway* and in the picture Buzz considered to be one of the best he ever made, *For Me and My Gal*, which co-starred the young Gene Kelly in his first film appearance.

Buzz didn't do so well with his own gals. He liked them pretty, not surprisingly, but Miss California may have been not too happy a choice. She didn't drink, so when she had a snifter to celebrate on the wedding night she passed out cold. Next morning she said she wanted to go home to mother, and Buzz duly put her on the plane. The marriage was annulled but the episode hardly helped his bank balance.

Busby Berkeley now moved back to Warners and decided he wanted to produce as well as direct. This is getting your foot in the front office and the front office folk don't like visitors. They agreed and signed, but then stalled. Unwisely, Buzz announced that he wanted to be released from his contract and Warners took him at his word. He went back to Broadway but his luck was running out. Not only did he marry—and soon divorce—a fourth lady, he seemed destined to become involved with money men who would discover they hadn't any. His mother died and the savings she had put away for him began to dwindle. He had to fall back upon the properties. The buyer always knows when you need a quick sale, and Buzz did, especially since the Inland Revenue had elected to come down on him for $120,000 in back taxes. For some reason he chose the moment to marry yet again.

When you are suicidally low, as Buzz confessed he was, the bottle has its attraction. Whether he took to it in a big way is not really known, but a small way is enough for the front office. Over uncertain ground Berkeley trekked, his pride deep in his pocket, back to Warner Brothers' studios. Jack Warner gave him the chance he needed, and before long he was working on Doris Day's first film. Louis B. Mayer, too, took him back when producer Arthur Freed wanted him to direct *Take Me out to the Ball Game*, which starred Esther Williams, Frank Sinatra and Gene Kelly.

Berkeley managed some superb aquatic numbers for other Esther Williams subjects and two numbers in the Cinemascope *Rose Marie*. In *Small Town Girl* he had Ann Miller dancing through an obstacle course of arms and instruments sticking up from the floor. He rehearsed her until her feet bled and she announced that she was going home. Her punishment was an early call next morning when she polished off the shot in one take.

The front office now became engaged in battle with television and the Berkeley sun began to set. His fifth marriage, which had lasted eight years, came to an end and his friend Etta Judd, now widowed, moved closely into his life. They married and remained devoted to one another. Offers were few and of doubtful quality: one Broadway show that proved to be under-financed; the excitement of a trip to Egypt—they actually travelled there for a picture to be financed by the Egyptian government. The collapse of this project was perhaps the biggest disappointment of all. Chuck Walters, an old friend, now gave Buzz his last assignment, and how he must have hated asking him to be his second unit director on the Doris Day picture *Jumbo*. It wasn't easy getting the approval of the front office, who gave it at last only on condition that he accepted a minimal down payment and the rest of his fee when he had completed his work.

Robert Lynd said: 'Every man of genius is considerably helped by being dead.' Busby Berkeley was very much alive but now became, ironically, a 'living legend'. 'A historical figure', they began to call him; 'an innovator in motion pictures' and, yet again, 'a genius'. He and Etta—with Ruby Keeler—were suddenly in demand to make personal appearances at colleges, universities and film institutes all over the world. The nostalgic sixties were in and it was revival time. There was one difference about this new nostalgia fashion: it lasted. Finally somebody in a front office somewhere had an idea: a revival on Broadway of the twenties' musical comedy *No, No, Nanette*. Who to star but Ruby Keeler, and who to supervise the production ... but the legendary seventy-four-year-old of whom Ruby Keeler had said: 'Hollywood is notorious for putting its pioneers out to pasture.'

No, No, Nanette opened in New York at the 46th Street Theatre on January 19th 1971. It was a rapturous evening, even the press surrendering to the occasion. One critic, Charles MacHarry of the *New York Daily News*, headed his notice 'Love Letter', and addressed it by name to all those principally concerned:

> Dear Busby Berkeley, Ruby Keeler, Jack Gilford, Patsy Kelly, Helen Gallagher, Bobby Van, the two pianos, the orchestra etc., whoever you are and everyone connected with Broadway's revival of 1925's *No, No, Nanette*... You, collectively, are darlings. I have never attended an opening night that generated more enthusiasm and may I say I whooped, applauded and otherwise cheered with all the others? I could not have been happier if I had been a backer...

It was a strange vindication; but stranger still that it should be needed.

Busby Berkeley will be remembered by us who were there when the magic first hit town; by youngers who marvel at television re-runs; by devotees who journey to see a showing at an out-of-town movie house; by those who are privy to the perennial delights of the National Film Theatre, to say nothing of the owners—if they are around and for as long as they are around—of 200 eager feet that danced on the screen in 1935 to *Lullaby of Broadway*. He will certainly forever be remembered by a schoolboy who grew up to be me.

COLE PORTER
Ace in the Hole

Cole Porter – a charcoal impression by Melik.

COLE PORTER

Cole Porter was born in the nineties just off Broadway. Broadway, Peru, Indiana, that is—a far cry from the Great White Way in New York. The date was June 9th 1892, though Cole, even in his early twenties, knocked off a couple of years. He had the reference books at variance and the biographers confused.

His grandfather had prospected for gold and found coal which is blacker but rich enough in its way. His daughter Kate Cole met one Samuel Fenwick Porter who didn't have a bean, let alone a coal mine. Not to undersell him, he did have a drug store. More important, Sam Porter had a winning way because Kate married him and brought him riches and a son whom they called Cole Albert.

Like the young Fats Waller, he had tremendous charm even when two feet tall—his eyes outdid those of Walt Disney's Bambi. Unlike those two other geniuses, Cole Porter was born wealthy. Grandad had swapped coal-mining for fruit and was farming 700 acres of it. Cole, of course, was a ripe plum for spoiling, but his genius was to show in that, dearly as he would love the playboy swim, he would strike out at will for deeper waters, and succeed in keeping his head above them at all times.

Young Cole took up the violin at six. Two years later he was alternating at the piano and composing his first ditty, 'Song of the birds', writing at the top: 'dedicated to my mother'. It was in two parts, 'Mother's cooing' and 'The young ones learning to sing'. His first published work, 'The Bobolink Waltz', appeared in his tenth year, 1902. The publisher didn't send him a copy, perhaps thinking that if he did he would have to give him a little money.

Our elders, of course, know what is best for us. Cole's millionaire grandfather saw Cole as a lawyer. His father, poor in dollars but rich in vision, gave him a taste for literature, in particular for the works of Browning. Cole went to Yale—where else? He didn't play football but he wrote songs about it which they rah-rah to this day. He was a cheer-leader and a member of everything you could join at Yale. The Pundits, for instance. The motto of the Pundits was the initial letters T.B.I.Y.T.B. They stood for 'The best is yet to be' from Browning's 'Rabbi Ben Ezra':

> Grow old along with me!
> The best is yet to be,
> The last of life, for which the first was made.

It worked better for Browning than it would for Cole. But in the early years it seemed life was his dozen of oysters, to say nothing of his champagne.

> Sturgeons thank God do it—
> Have some caviare, dear . . .

The days around him, the years ahead—like the fountain of youth which in a lyric he described as a mixture of gin and vermouth, would surely be everlasting.

In 1913 Cole graduated from Yale and, dutifully, began to study at Harvard Law School. It was the Dean who suggested he abandon it in favour of music. To the Harvard School of Music he went and collaborated—for the first and only time—with Lawrason Riggs on *See America First*, a musical comedy in the style of Gilbert and Sullivan. It was produced on Broadway in 1916, starring Clifton Webb; two weeks later it closed. What do you do when your hopes go up in a closure notice after so short a lease? Clifton Webb—it was his first Broadway show too—stuck around. Cole Porter left for France to join the Foreign Legion, not, it seems, the dreaded Legion of P. C. Wren and Beau Geste nor even the Legion Stan Laurel joined because Hardy wanted to forget, but an amiable kind of Legion. Cole was allowed to march carrying a piano on his back. At least it looked like a piano, in fact it was a zither with a piano keyboard. His fellow soldiers, relishing the prospect of entertainment, were not averse to sharing the burden.

The war was going great guns but Cole didn't see much of it. He wrote a parody of the Kern and Harbach song 'They didn't believe me' that ran:

AND WHEN THEY ASK US HOW DANGEROUS IT WAS
WE NEVER WILL TELL THEM, WE NEVER WILL TELL THEM
HOW WE FOUGHT IN SOME CAFE WITH WILD WOMEN
    NIGHT AND DAY,
'TWAS THE WONDERF'LEST WAR YOU EVER KNEW;
AND WHEN THEY ASK US, AND THEY'RE CERTAINLY GOING TO
    ASK US
WHY ON OUR CHESTS WE DO NOT WEAR
    THE CROIX DE GUERRE . . .
WE NEVER WILL TELL THEM, WE NEVER WILL TELL THEM
THERE WAS A FRONT—BUT DAMNED IF WE KNEW WHERE.

Cole did teach a bit of gunnery to the American troops, and may have bumped into Busby Berkeley who was engaged in the same thing. But in his off-duty moments—and these were, so to speak, legion—it was party time at his luxurious Paris apartment. He met a wealthy divorcee—a gay one too, in the old sense of the word. She was Linda Lee Thomas, beautiful, elegant and a superb hostess.

Cole the rich boy was able to trip back and forth across the Atlantic as other folk of the day crossed the road. Not yet by plane, but by the slower, more pleasant way: ocean voyages on luxurious liners. On one of these he met Raymond Hitchcock who was giving his name, or part of it, annually to revues to be presented on Broadway. He engaged Cole to write the score for *Hitchy Koo of 1919*. The show was a success and Cole had his first 'standard', a song called 'Old-Fashioned Garden'. It was only a step away from 'That old-fashioned mother of mine', not very Porterish, but it gave you the feeling you had heard it before which in turn made you want to hear it again which, of course, is what makes a standard.

Back in Paris, Cole's playboy world was astonished by the announcement of his forthcoming marriage to Linda. His circle of friends was largely made up of what was politely referred to as 'perennial bachelors'. How would they take this new gambit? How would Cole take it? The Upper Bracket, we should have known, takes everything in its stride. It isn't really done to bat an eyelid—paint it, yes, brush the lashes with mascara, but bat it, never.

The Cole Porters—'Les Colporteurs' to the Parisians—set up permanent house at Numéro 13 in the Rue Monsieur. Cole wasn't short of a franc but his grandfather, who didn't think much of music and lyric writing, was keeping him on relatively short rations—which meant that the champagne was served not in Jereboams but in mere magnums. Linda's wealth proved to be useful, especially when it came to such gestures as engaging the entire Monte Carlo Ballet to entertain your friends. Yet—and here we remember Carlyle's definition of genius as 'a transcendent capacity of taking trouble'—Cole studied diligently under Vincent D'Indy, finding hours that weren't on the clock. He described his work schedule to an interviewer who set it out in this way. 'Three or four parties a night, a wink of sleep between sun-up and ten a.m. and then a stretch of work from eleven a.m. to five p.m. when he starts the gay night life again.' Added to this, the parties—or party, it was really one unending round—extended itself all about Europe. Party time might chime in Paris, on the Rhine, or on the Riviera.

In Venice the Porters rented the Rezzonico Palace where Browning had lived and died. Along would come Noel Coward, Cecil Beaton—perennial bachelors both—and another, Monty Woolley, who'd been with Cole at Yale and would later win theatre and film fame as *The Man Who Came to Dinner*. Edward, Prince of Wales was a guest, and so was the famous 'hostess with the mostes' ', Elsa Maxwell. Cole scandalized the Venice Lido by introducing a floating night club with a band of musicians led by the incomparable Hutch.

In 1923 (presumably with an ice pack on his young head) he composed his first and last serious work, a ballet for the Swiss Ballet Company. It was a hit in Paris and on its American tour and it encouraged Cole's friend George Gershwin who, after only a few months, produced his *Rhapsody in Blue*. Cole had had two bits of advice. Irving Berlin told him to skip the travel, to stick closer to 42nd Street and Broadway. Elsa Maxwell said to him: 'Your standards are too high ...' She didn't suggest he lower them. 'One day,' she said, 'you will haul the public up to your own level and then the world will be yours...'

In 1924 Cole contributed some songs to *The Greenwich Village Follies* but had no luck. Then one day, on a beach in Venice, he met Ray Goetz the producer. Goetz wanted a composer to write songs with a Parisian flavour for his show to be called *Paris*. Irene Bordoni would be the star. The score for *Paris*, which opened in 1928, included one of Cole Porter's classic songs, 'Let's do it'.

Cole and Linda Porter now moved back to New York for good. Not exactly at 42nd Street and Broadway but the Porter equivalent, Fifth Avenue. Ironically, his next show—*Wake up and Dream*, produced in 1929—was for Charles B. Cochran in London. Its hit song was 'What is this thing called love?' *Fifty Million Frenchmen* happened in the same year. Through the thunder of the market crash Porter's smooth music and smoother lyrics made themselves heard, and he may, for all one knows, have stopped the odd ruined stockholder from jumping off a window ledge. He was becoming one of the top song writers of the day—a song writer in the true sense of the term; Kern was a composer, Hammerstein a lyricist. Cole Porter was one of the rare few who wrote both, and it takes both to make a song.

In 1930, in *The New Yorkers*, Cole proved—not for the first time—that his lyrical drift was way ahead of both public thinking and censorship. 'Love for sale' he wrote in his beloved minor key. It was a minor-key subject:

IF YOU WANT TO BUY MY WARES
FOLLOW ME AND CLIMB THE STAIRS . . .

In 1933 I was playing juveniles (and other things—I was also Emily Brontë's dog off stage) in the Birmingham Repertory Company. I was keen on the juvenile girl, who happened to own a portable gramophone and a couple of 78s. Listening to these records after the performance at the Rep and over late-night cornflakes in the Pershore Road, I was introduced to the magic of Cole Porter. *Nymph Errant* had just opened in London and Gertrude Lawrence had recorded a song that cost Porter a whole lost weekend, closeted with a medical dictionary. The lyric fascinated me. 'He said my maxillaries were marvels', I was convinced, meant something beautiful. Cole had this way of fooling you.

Nymph Errant, for no good reason, was never played on Broadway, but we loved it in the Pershore Road. Gordon Cryer was Stage Manager at the Birmingham Rep at that time—he was later to develop as someone important at the B.B.C. Like everyone else but me, Gordon had a portable gramophone, and one day he brought it into my dressing room tucked under one arm. Carefully carried in both hands he had a 78. 'I don't know what you'll think of this,' he said, 'I won't tell you what I think until you've heard it ...' 'What is it?' I asked, daubing my face with a stick of Leichner grease paint. 'Cole Porter's latest, it's from *The Gay Divorce*. The show's coming to the Royal up the road in a couple of weeks.' 'I know,' I said, 'we're all going to the matinée.' 'Yes,' said Gordon. 'This is the hit song. And it's all on one note ... to begin with, anyway. Listen and then tell me what you think.' I did. 'It's terrific,' I said. 'I think so too,' he said. Two weeks later we, along with the whole company, sat enraptured as Fred Astaire sang 'Night and Day' on the stage.

By now I was a mad Cole Porter fan. Although he was a generation ahead of me he seemed to embody all that we youngers felt and were striving for, and expressed it musically and lyrically. His cynicism suited us—me, certainly—better than Noël Coward's. Noël's was a down beat comment. I was too young to understand his Twentieth Century Blues, to sympathize with his Parisian Pierrot whose spirits were zero—unlike mine. Porter, though he was older than Coward, had, I think, benefited as a writer from being affluent. He had the gift of making you want to rise to heights yourself rather than envying the mountaineering skill of others and wanting to pull them off the peak. You wanted to be rich, certainly, but you wanted the achievement too, not merely the perks of the peaks. He invited us all to the party, the one that wasn't supposed to end.

By the following year, we Birmingham Repsters were in London, trying to find work. *Anything Goes* opened at the Palace Theatre and I was there. In New York Ethel Merman had trumpeted the lead; in London, Charles Cochran had cast the gentler French star Jeanne Aubert. Though some people, including the odd critic, didn't like her, I fell for her hook, line and sinker. *Anything Goes* had a scoreful of hits, the title song, 'Blow, Gabriel Blow', 'All through the night', and 'You're the top', the 'catalogue song' to begin and end them all. Cockie mentioned to Cole that certain of his lyrics might not be understood by the British. In the first verse, for instance, the singer apologizes for the quality . . .

> AT WORDS POETIC, I'M SO PATHETIC
> THAT I OFTEN HAVE FOUND IT BEST . . .

and notice the quadruple rhyming . . .

> INSTEAD OF GETTING THEM OFF MY CHEST,
> TO LET 'EM REST UNEXPRESSED . . .

That's understandable enough. But in the second verse the girl answers, saying, 'That's all right, you're doing fine . . .'—or as Porter has it:

> THOSE OTHERS HUMANS LIKE VINCENT YOUMANS
> MIGHT THINK THAT YOUR SONG IS BAD . . .

No, No, Nanette had played the same theatre nine years earlier and the town would sing 'Tea for two' for ever but, sadly, we have to ask: would they know the name of the man who wrote the melody? Porter was always happy to meet such a challenge. For London, he had Jeanne Aubert change 'Youmans' for 'Novello'—rhyming him with 'fellow', moreover. For good measure he buttered up Cochran by mentioning his famous 'Young Ladies'. He did call them a 'chorus' which took the edge off . . . and he rhymed them with 'Brontosaurus'.

Jubilee, in 1935, had one of Cole's very best songs, but it wasn't to come to wide notice until Artie Shaw recorded it three years later. When he did, 'Begin the Beguine' joined the immortal ranks. In late 1935 Cole and Linda took the Golden Road to the celluloid Samarkand called Hollywood. Strangely, Linda—the hostess to rival Elsa Maxwell, and prettier with it—hated the movie colony. Cole, on the other hand, to quote Dorothy Kilgallen, 'went Hollywood quickly and completely'. 'I like it here,' he said to her. 'It's like living on the moon, isn't it? When I first came here they told me you'll be so bored you'll die. Nobody talks about anything but pictures. After I was here a week, I discovered I didn't want to talk about anything else myself...'

Born to Dance, starring Eleanor Powell and James Stewart, was Cole's first film, for MGM. Stewart told me about going round to Cole's house to hear the song he was to sing in the picture. He hadn't much of a voice and 'Easy to love' wasn't easy to sing. 'Can't you bring the music down?' asked Jimmy. 'No,' said Cole. 'Let's bring the voice up.' They did decide to dub the singing later, but at the preview Jimmy was surprised still to hear his own voice, croaky but quite pleasant. They left it. As Jimmy stammered it to me, 'The song was so good, I guess they thought even I couldn't ruin it.'

In 1937 Cole Porter was able to boast that he had made Louis B. Mayer cry. Mind you, this wasn't difficult; he was known to water easily at the eyes, especially when he wasn't getting his absolute way with a star. 'In the still of the night' did it in this instance. Cole wrote it for *Rosalie*. He wrote the title song six times to satisfy himself, and then had to write a seventh version for Mayer. Mayer didn't cry this time but Cole did, privately, at what he considered to be the banality of the forced treatment. It was a hit and Irving Berlin congratulated Cole. Cole told him: 'Thanks a lot, but I wrote that song in hate and I still hate it.' Berlin answered: 'Listen kid, take my advice, never hate a song that has sold half a million copies.'

Hollywood, not for the first time, took its matrimonial toll. The Porter marriage began, discreetly, to open at the seams. Linda was in Europe when Cole, now back in New York, attended a weekend party at which his 'Ridin' high' song, so recently written, would have a ghastly echo. The scene was fitting enough—the exclusive Piping Rock Club in Locust Valley, Long Island. It was Cole's idea that they should go riding. He was out of practice and the groom advised him against the spirited horse he chose. But Cole was in a mood to be adamant. His mount shied at a fence and fell back. Cole didn't manage to slip the stirrups in time and the horse rolled on him, crushing one of his legs. It tried to get up, fell back again and crushed his other leg. The reaction was typically Upper Bracket. 'When the horse fell on me,' he said later, 'I was too stunned to be conscious of great pain. Until help came I worked on the lyrics for a song called 'At long last love'.

IS IT AN EARTHQUAKE . . .? (He wrote)
OR SIMPLY A SHOCK?
IS IT THE GOOD TURTLE SOUP OR MERELY THE MOCK . . .?
IS IT A COCKTAIL, THIS FEELING OF JOY . . .?
OR IS WHAT I FEEL THE REAL MCCOY . . .?

He was able, at this moment, to belittle his work . . .

HAVE I THE RIGHT HUNCH OR HAVE I THE WRONG?
WILL IT BE BACH I HEAR OR JUST A COLE PORTER SONG?

Preparing for the film *Broadway Melody of 1940*. Cole with Fred
Astaire and Eleanor Powell.

The smoothly progressing dream was over. Or was it? Was it merely the smooth progress he would never know again? The surgeons would have amputated both legs but Linda cabled 'No decision until I arrive.' It was a staggering fact that she had had the same decision to make in the case of her ex-husband. And they had been separated at the time. Linda had refused to allow amputation and had nursed him to complete recovery. Back she came now to Cole's side where she would stay until she died seventeen years later. For Cole, life would be longer—much longer. It would seem an eternity.

The years that now began would be dominated by bandages, leg-irons, sticks, crutches, wheelchairs. There would be more than thirty operations on his legs, attempts to save them, and finally, after more than twenty years, an operation to remove his right leg. No comfort for the elegant playboy who had made us all millionaires by proxy. He didn't really disdain the fountain of youth—it was chic and amusing to describe it as a mixture of gin and vermouth. Somehow, too, in the cynicism, there was a courage that he communicated to us all. It wasn't his way to complain about the disasters of reality, it wasn't the done thing to acknowledge its existence; you must play against it, play against it all the way.

Cole wrote a song once that spoke of reserves and of what a good thing it is to have them:

> ALWAYS HAVE AN ACE IN THE HOLE (it said)...
> SAD TIMES MAY FOLLOW YOUR TRACKS,
> BAD TIMES MAY BAR YOU FROM SACHS...

Sachs, Fifth Avenue, was a pricey emporium, but bad times would never bar the Cole Porters from shopping there. Yet Cole didn't 'write down' to the extent of suggesting they might bar *us* from shopping anywhere less pricey. He was pulling us up to his financial level and we loved him for the flattery.

His recovery, although that can hardly be the right word, began with two years in hospital. One 'ace in the hole' he produced was a new-style piano, which he had constructed. It spanned his bed, like one of those contraptions that support breakfast.

The score for *Leave it to Me* in 1938 had a newcomer named Gene Kelly supporting a newcomer named Mary Martin. When she assured us that her 'Heart belonged to Daddy' it was made comfortingly clear that Cole Porter hadn't lost his touch. In the same show the composer/lyricist harped on a favourite theme, the disparagement of his own sex. The song 'I hate men' would come later, but here he mentioned that 'Most gentlemen don't like love—they just like to kick it around'. One section of the lyric is filled with both warning and beautiful alliteration...

AS MADAME SAPPHO IN SOME SONNET SAID,
A SLAP AND A TICKLE IS ALL THAT THE FICKLE
MALE EVER HAD IN HIS HEAD...

... and we may not miss the subtlety in that it was Madame Sappho who said it.

In the following year, 1939, Cole wrote words and music for a movie that was to have been 'Broadway Melody' of that year but turned out to be 'Broadway Melody of 1940'.

Dubarry was a Lady which opened in December of '39 was the last Broadway Musical of the decade. Bert Lahr was Louis XV and Ethel Merman his unlikely Dubarry. A youngster named Betty Grable was in it too, making her first Broadway appearance. Cole and the show did one another proud. 'Do I love you, do I? Doesn't one and one make two?', 'Katie went to Haiti'—we used to rhyme one with the other—and we learned that 'Katie knew her Haiti, and practically all Haiti knew Katie'; 'Well did you evah', the song that later graced the movie *High Society*; a typical Porter catalogue song 'But in the morning' no!' with lyrics that confounded the censor:

SHE: ARE YOU FOND OF SWIMMING, DEAR,
       KINDLY TELL ME IF SO . . .
 HE: YES, I'M FOND OF SWIMMING, DEAR,
       BUT IN THE MORNING, NO!
       WHEN THE SUN, THRO' THE BLIND
       STARTS TO BURN MY POOR BEHIND,
       THAT'S THE TIME WHEN I'M IN LOW . . .
SHE: DO YOU USE THE BREAST STROKE, DEAR?
 HE: YES, I USE THE BREAST STROKE, DEAR
       BUT IN THE MORNING, NO!

There's a chorus about accountancy . . .

ARE YOU GOOD AT FIGURES, DEAR? . . .

In which she progresses to:

DO YOU DO DOUBLE ENTRY?

Not in the morning, he sings.
Some of the releases—or middle bits—are Porter personified . . .

WHEN THE MAID TODDLES IN WITH MY ORANGE JUICE
AND GIN . . .

or:

WHEN I START WITH A FROWN, READING WINCHELL
UPSIDE DOWN . . .

Marvellous descriptions—from life—of hangover mornings . . .
The pearl of the couplets, for me is:

DO YOU LIKE MIAMI, DEAR—KINDLY TELL ME IF SO . . .

YES, I LIKE YOUR AMI, DEAR . . . BUT IN THE MORNING NO!

Dubarry was a Lady hit London in wartime and took our minds off other things that were being aimed. The definitive rendering of one song came to us later when Johnny Mercer joined Judy Garland to record 'Friendship'.

The friendship that is an essential ingredient in marriage continued between Cole and his wife. They had been separated at the time of his accident but now she was always there to give him support as one physical trial followed another. She had arranged the sale of their house in Paris, with understanding. How do you take a man back to a scene where he was king-pin playboy and ask him to sit musing in a wheelchair? In the spring of 1940 the Porters bought an estate called Buxton Hill in Massachusetts. It was vast, beautiful and had a swimming-pool. In avoidance of cruelty to yourself, you don't penalize your friends; both Cole and Linda knew this, and a swimming-pool there was. How Cole would have loved it all just three years earlier!

Cole pretended that his ace in the hole was all he needed, the inner resources. Carried into the theatre by two hired strong men, he—publicly—had a ball at his first nights. And into some of his verses poured the determination to laugh away sorrow with a quip. *Panama Hattie* had a lyric that ran:

> ONCE I OWNED A TREASURE SO RARE, SO PURE . . .
> THE GREATEST OF TREASURES—
> HAPPINESS SAFE AND SECURE . . .
> BUT LIKE EVERY HOPE TOO RASH,
> MY TREASURE, I FIND, IS TRASH . . .
> SO MAKE IT ANOTHER OLD FASHIONED, PLEASE . . .

Let's Face It, a Broadway 1943 offering, had that 'Ace in the hole' song. In the same year Cole scored the movie *Something to Shout About*. The Porter penchant for pre-sending up a romantic chorus with a quip-filled verse was indulged again in a beautiful minor-key ballad. 'It's not . . .' he says in the verse, '. . . that

you're rarer than asparagus out of season. No, my darling, this is
the reason why you've got to be mine . . . YOU'D BE SO NICE
TO COME HOME TO . . .'

Something for the Boys was Cole Porter's second Broadway
opening in '43 . . . *Mexican Hayride* and *Seven Lively Arts* he
offered in '44 . . . 'Every Time We Say Goodbye,' he wrote . . .

THERE'S NO LOVE SONG FINER
BUT HOW STRANGE THE CHANGE FROM MAJOR TO MINOR . . .

He loved 'major to minor' musically and he can't have missed the
analogy with life as some folk have to live it.

In 1948 he scored *The Pirate*, a movie that starred Gene Kelly
and Judy Garland. He also scored *Kiss Me, Kate* for the stage.
They weren't even going to ask Cole to undertake it. 'He's too
ill,' they said. 'Written out,' they said, 'He's sick, he's finished
. . .' He had, creatively—it seemed—barely begun. *Kiss Me Kate*,
based very loosely on Shakespeare's *The Taming of the Shrew*,
opened in December of 1948 and ran for more than a thousand
performances. It contained so many top songs: 'Where is the life
that once I led?'; 'Always true to you in my fashion', with the
Spooneristic 'If A Harris pat means a Paris hat—O.K.!'—Cole
wrote chorus after chorus to that, and to 'Too darn hot'. Yet
again he proved that he was at his romantic happiest in the minor
key with 'So in love' which could be considered one of his very
best songs.

Two gangsters threaten Petruchio backstage. They are also a
lyrical threat to the Bard in a brilliant song in which they set out
to brush him up. The sensitive censor worried again about
Porter's gift for innocent thin-ice skating. Innocent? Either way
they regarded him as something of a pain in the arts. But what
can you do with such triple entendre as:

IF SHE SAYS YOUR BEHAVIOUR IS HEINOUS
KICK HER HARD IN THE CORIOLANUS . . .?

After *Kiss Me, Kate*, many another writer of words and music

would have rested on his laurels. Porter scored *Out of Nowhere*—
to open in 1950. When you write a lyric that has lines like 'From
this moment on ... no more blue songs—only whoop-de-doo
songs ...' and set it in the minor key, could it be you are
expressing a doubt in the matter? Cynicism for home consump-
tion? In the same show Porter had a beautiful ballad which for
once was cast very much in the major key—the positiveness of
the lyric demanded it. Out with cynicism here...

> I AM LOVED . . . ABSOLUTELY LOVED . . .
> WHAT A WONDERFUL THING TO BE ABLE TO SAY . . .!

Leaving aside the devotion of his wife Linda, the public took
Cole Porter to heart every time his pen went to work to produce a
song for them to sing when at play. Porter, who no longer was
one, could make playboys of us all. It is to be hoped he felt the
glow of the warmth he generated.

Can-Can opened in May of 1953. In it Porter celebrated his
favourite city all over again in a minor-changing-to major piece
called simply 'I love Paris'. Cole Porter now was making a routine
of spending his summers in California. In July of '53 he received
a letter from Irving Berlin: 'Dear Cole ... Elizabeth (my
youngest) and I went to see *Can-Can* last night and, along with a
packed house of satisfied customers, we loved it. It's a swell show
and I still say, to paraphrase an old bar-room ballad, Anything I
can do you can do better ... Love, Irving...'

The movie of *Can-Can* starred Frank Sinatra, who was
something of a worry to Cole. Cole hated the twistings and
additions to his lyrics. Once, at a party, he made this clear when
the singer interpreted 'I get a kick out of you'. Now, for Porter
himself to write against the sentiment with such lines as:

> SOME GET A KICK FROM COCAINE . . .
> I'M SURE THAT IF I TOOK EVEN ONE SNIFF
> THAT WOULD BORE ME TERRIFIC'LLY TOO . . .
> YET I GET A KICK OUT OF YOU.

was on the sophisticated target. For a singer to express it with the added phrase 'You Give Me a Boot' was less acceptable. *Can-Can* had nearly 900 Broadway performances.

During the run and while Cole was working on the score for *Silk Stockings*, Linda Porter died. Cole was alone and in despair. In the following year he moved into a specially designed and decorated nine-room apartment at the Waldorf Towers in New York. It was on the thirty-third floor. But his friends were forcibly reminded of a lyric Cole had written a year before his accident in 1936, the more so because of his nowadays inability to live it up and forget at night spots like Jack and Charlie's 21 and El Morocco . . .

WHILE THE CROWDS AT EL MOROCCO PUNISH THE PARQUET
AND AT TWENTY-ONE THE COUPLES CLAMOUR FOR MORE . . .
I'M DESERTED AND DEPRESSED
IN MY REGAL EAGLE NEST . . .
DOWN IN THE DEPTHS ON THE NINETIETH FLOOR . . .

Silk Stockings opened in November of 1954. It extolled the joys of a free, capitalist society where the drinks are hard and the lingerie soft.

In 1956 MGM invited Cole to write the score for *High Society*. Sinatra had played in the screen version of *Can-Can*, and now Porter had him again. But he also had Bing Crosby, Louis Armstrong and Grace Kelly. Under heavy direction from the MGM Front Office he produced for Crosby and Kelly what he himself considered one of his most banal pieces. 'True love' was hardly a Porter title before you start; it proved to be one of his most successful songs, so somebody was right.

Porter was asked to write a duet for Crosby and Sinatra. This hurdle seemed insurmountable, so he didn't try to surmount it. He lifted 'Well did you evah, what a swell party this is' from his earlier show, *Dubarry was a Lady*. A very un-typical Porter song was the one he wrote for Bing and Satchmo—un-typical not, in this case, because he didn't want to write it. He had enormous fun creating and playing 'That's jazz' for demonstration. This time, he allowed and revelled in the brilliant and tasteful ad libs by the two masters of the skill. But the basic song was all Cole. When you set the life and ebullience of 'That's jazz' against the situation of the man who wrote it, the driving force of genius is the only possible answer.

From time to time, throughout his career, Cole would delight his friends with the odd party song which would then filter out to public hearing. 'Miss Otis regrets she's unable to lunch today', he dedicated to Elsa Maxwell. Then there was the song about the hostess with the leastes', Mrs Louseborough-Goodby:

THANK YOU SO MUCH
FOR THOSE COCKTAILS SO HOT
AND THE BATH THAT WAS NOT . . .
FOR THE PTOMAINE I GOT FROM YOUR FAMOUS
TINNED SALMON,
FOR THE FORTUNE I LOST WHEN YOU TAUGHT ME
BACKGAMMON . . .

One beautiful couplet runs:

THANK YOU A LOT MRS LOUSEBORO'-GOODBY,
THANK YOU A LOT . . .
AND DON'T BE SURPRISED IF YOU SUDDENLY SHOULD BE
QUIETLY SHOT . . .

A song Cole wrote in 1934, surely with tongue-in-cowboy-cheek, was sung in 1944 in a movie called *Hollywood Canteen* by Roy Rogers, the producers having taken the song at face value.

GIVE ME LAND, LOTS OF LAND . . . DON'T FENCE ME IN . . .

may be all right for singing on a horse, but what about 'Take me out where the west commences'? Not exactly words that would trip off the tongue of, say, John Wayne. 'Wunderbar' in *Kiss Me, Kate* is a Porter send up. Like 'True love' it is taken at face value by many hearers, though even at face value, 'Wunderbar' is attractive. It seems that, try as he might—even with a film mogul breathing inartistically down his neck—Cole Porter found it impossible to write a bad song.

The pain and the loneliness began to take over. He had written the score for a television version of *Aladdin* when he went into hospital for amputation. When he was well again—whatever that might mean—he began to withdraw into himself. As Linda had guessed so many years ago, the pride in his body had been finally shattered. His seventieth birthday was celebrated by a revival of *Anything Goes* at the Orpheum Theatre, down town N.Y. Elsa Maxwell presided but Cole, by now a total recluse, didn't attend. In the summer of 1964 he made his usual journey to California. There he had one more operation, this time for the removal of a kidney stone. It wasn't a major operation and there were no complications, but he died in hospital on October 15th.

Cole was forty-five years old at the time of his accident. He had endured to seventy-two. His genius had insisted on his continuing, it seemed. What beautiful work! But at what a cost! He had left instructions that no great fuss should be made, and was buried in his home town, Peru, Indiana, where he lies between his mother and his wife Linda.

Cole Albert Porter . . . the rich boy who gave us riches, was reared in the lap of so much luxury that you would expect him to be spoiled. Indeed he was. He was fun loving, yet he had, somewhere deep down, an iron strength. Maybe the fate that put it there knew it would be called upon to the very full. If anybody ever needed a personal ace in the hole, it was Cole Porter.

MAURICE CHEVALIER
From the French

Maurice, aged 65, in a solo performance – building Colette's 'invisible bridge of atoms' to reach his audience.

MAURICE CHEVALIER

In the year 1888 Paris was preparing for the Great Exhibition which would open the following year and would herald the glittering decade known in England as the Gay Nineties, in France as *la Belle Epoque*. The Eiffel Tower was all but complete. On the night of September 12th they tried out the electricity, and the tower was lit up for the first time. You could see it all the way to Menilmontant, the slum village on the hillside where earlier that same day Maurice Auguste Chevalier had been born. In the words of Jean Cocteau, 'France has two monuments—the Eiffel Tower and Maurice Chevalier. She loves them both dearly.'

The Chevalier children were ten in number, of whom seven died in infancy. Maurice was the youngest of three surviving sons. His mother Josephine was a frail, hard-working woman, his father a hopeless alcoholic who walked out—or staggered out—for good when Maurice was eight years old. The oldest boy, Charles, did his best but at last married and moved away and the second brother Paul became head of the family trio, bringing in three francs a day.

Maurice, at the age of nine, would shovel snow when he should have been at school so that, at the end of the day, he might carry home to his mother the odd franc. Once he was able to give her a Christmas present, a newly baked loaf of bread. The smell was irresistible. Also he could warm his hands on it as he carried it up the hill.

Josephine Chevalier had an all-night job as a cleaning woman In the daytime, instead of sleeping, she made lace. When at last she collapsed and was moved to a charity hospital, Paul had to send Maurice to an orphanage on the other side of Paris. The day came when mother called for him to take him home and the busy round began again. Things were better by now. Paul was a fully-fledged engraver earning forty-two francs a week. Maurice, at eleven, left school and became an apprentice at Paul's foundary.

Every week the Chevaliers went to the circus and Maurice conceived the idea of becoming an acrobat. He passed his enthusiasm to Paul and they practised nightly at the local gym. Maurice took to day-dreaming about somersaults and got the sack from the foundry. Paul, as the breadwinner, threw in the acrobatic towel, bread being all too hard to win, but Maurice got a job with the Cirque d'Hiver as an understudy, without pay—which represented a drop from what he had picked up snow-clearing. As a mere actor I must say that it wouldn't have occurred to me to think of acrobats having understudies. He had to rehearse, of course . . . and fell off a high wire. It damaged his pelvis and, more permanently, his ambitions in the field of physical leaps and bounds. He was twelve and a bit.

Maurice continued to day-dream about being an entertainer of sorts and lost job after job. Such mooning conflicted with carpentry, electrics, making pens . . . mixing paint in a doll factory and painting the dolls' faces . . . It interfered seriously with the task of making drawing pins; he caught his thumb in the machinery and changed the shape of it. Years later someone asked him whether his damaged thumb was a worry to him and he answered: 'Only when I want to unbutton a lady in a hurry . . .'

Maurice adored his mother. He and Paul named her 'La Louque', a name which he would later give his villa. The word has mystified biographers, but in fact it has no meaning outside the family. Paul took Mama and Maurice to the Café des Trois Lions where they saw and heard singers and comedians. 'This is what you should have tried,' his mother said, 'the worst that can happen here is a rotten tomato . . .' A rotten tomato seed is what she planted that night—Maurice determined to become a Music

Hall entertainer. He learned a song and got 'La Louque' to run him up a costume. The manager at the Trois Lions was willing to give him a chance; the Chevaliers were regulars, and he thought regulars might put up with regulars. Maurice sang like a frenzied if unqualified lark but in a different key from the pianist. He was a riot but not a success.

A professional named Gilbert suggested Maurice take singing lessons. How do you pay for singing lessons in Menilmontant? Your mother makes lace, seems to have been the answer—the teacher's daughter had a fully embroidered trousseau by the time Maurice was ready to try again. He was better. Not good but definitely better. He began to get small, short-lived engagements—the Tourelles Casino, La Ville Japonaise, the Casino de Montmartre, La Fourmi . . . His performances were broad, even crude. The boy put his hands in his pockets and hitched up his breeches to show what manhood he had. Some in the audiences guffawed, others shouted their disgust. He was learning the hardest possible way.

He acquired an agent who actually found work for him. It was as well because Paul married and Maurice became the breadwinner. He and his mother moved into an apartment in the middle of the café activity to await engagements—and bread. Sometimes it was the merest crust, at others the crust was smeared with the cheapest of near-butters. Now and again they had a glass of wine. Maurice continued to visit the gymnasium. The need for self-defence in the region led to his becoming quite a boxer. On stage he mimicked the great Music Hall stars of the day and earned for himself a reputation as an accentric comedian. He didn't think of changing his grotesque style, but rather perfected it, and was soon in demand all over France. He was eighteen when Sarah Bernhardt made a journey to see him at the Alcazar in Marseilles. In Lyons he met Colette who immortalized him—before he accomplished that for himself—in her novel *La Vagabonde*. Mistinguett, whom he had approached to express his admiration after a performance in Paris, wrote:

I recognized him three or four years later in a little night club in Montmartre where he was doing a cabaret turn. I watched him work, it was a revelation. He put the song over as if he were humming it to himself for his own pleasure, with a rhythm and sureness of touch that took my breath away. His get-up had to be seen to be believed. A blue and white striped sailor jersey, a skimpy jacket and a bowler hat which he used to startling effect. I met him again when he was playing at the Variétés where he often came. We used to pass each other on the stairs, he smiled and I smiled back. He called me plain 'Mistinguett' and I called him 'Chevalier'. When I took up my employ as Mistress of Ceremonies at the Folies Bergères with the girls, the boys, the ostrich feathers and the inevitable staircase I found to my delight that Maurice was also in the cast . . .

'Also' is a word not beloved of actors. According to Maurice, Mistinguett was also there. She became his mistress but he remained in control.

The British Tiller Girls appeared in Paris and sang an American song. Maurice was impressed with the new rhythm and travelled to London where he saw *Hullo Ragtime* at the Hippodrome. The American star Elsie Janis was happy enough to meet him. She invited him to appear with her in her next London show but Maurice protested his lack of English. 'You have something no Englishman can match,' she said. 'Gallic charm.' It gave him food for Gallic thought. Something else did too—the show itself. *Hullo Ragtime* had men appearing as themselves—no short jackets and bowler hats, no eccentricity.

For the first time in this century the Germans played *Gott* and Europe was turned inside out. Careers went by the draft board. Maurice had joined in 1913 for his two years of military service but when the Germans invaded France the action moved away from the parade ground. In his first foray Maurice collected the Croix de Guerre and a lump of lead in his chest. He was also captured, and lingered in a prisoner of war camp. It was in a jail of sorts that Louis Armstrong learned to play the trumpet. In this jail Maurice learned to speak and to sing in English. A fellow prisoner was a teacher from Newcastle named Ronald Kennedy, and when his pupil left the camp he spoke English as well as would ever be necessary for Maurice Chevalier.

An exchange of prisoners was arranged by the Red Cross and Maurice found himself in Paris. He was invalided out of the army and soon was back with Mistinguett at the Folies Bergères. Their success was such that Maurice demanded equal billing. When this was denied him the partnership—on stage and off—came to an end. As Mistinguett put it: 'Our success had no doubt gone to Maurice's head a bit. He stopped calling for me at the end of the performance as he had done every night without fail for years . . .'

Maurice saw it differently: 'In spite of her sincere love Mist always considered me just a foil for her great talent. She never thought of me as an equal on the stage or as a rival. This saddened me. I could see no solution. I loved Mist . . . but I adored my profession.'

In 1919 Owen Nares announced that he would leave the cast of *Hullo America* at the Palace Theatre in London. Maurice sent a wire to Nares' co-star, Elsie Janis again, to ask if he might take over. Mistinguett had given Maurice a certain schooling in romantic know-how, on and off stage. His prison camp instructor had taught him the rudiments of English; Elsie Janis now took up the instruction, both branches of it, night and day. She taught him how to shape a phrase in the new language, how to use the Gallic charm in a song. Singing was never Maurice's forte but such was the charm you didn't mind. It wasn't only charm, however; he lived a song, took you along with him, made you live it too. He was careful never to learn English too well. After more than fifty years at it he preserved the same degree of accent—it was very good business.

Back in Paris he played the Casino with Mistinguett. He required equal billing, got it, and as a result it was now Mistinguett who walked out. The confident manager removed her name from the marquee and starred Maurice solo. Chevalier's style had undergone a radical change. He was no longer the eccentric. He now appeared in a tuxedo and wearing a straw hat—and his own personality. To the French he was France, to the Parisians, Paris.

Every aspect of Gallic life came into his songs. At the time the Place Pigalle was the centre of the red light district—and the red light was legal. It was when I first went to Paris as a lad and I must say everything was superbly under control. As with prohibition, later restraint led only to crime and the debasement of the merchandise. There were street helpers who wanted to sell you this and that, point the way to a better evening. Maurice delighted Paris with a song that included the patter: 'You're a foreigner? You want to buy flowers? A gramme of cocaine...?' 'Risqué' was the word the English used at that time. Anything French was liable to be 'near the knuckle'. We envied it, popped over to Paris to indulge in it but frowned upon it with the hypocrisy of which we have always been inordinately proud. I achieved a special popularity at school when it was known that I owned a full-page colour picture of Josephine Baker as appearing at the Folies Bergères. Nowadays Europeans, even Americans who gave strip tease to the world, come over to England, where what we have to offer is dirtier and not nearly as attractive.

Chevalier appeared with huge success in the operetta *Dédé* which ran for two years. He began filming in the daytime—silent filming. Such round-the-clockery has put paid to many an artist, and Chevalier began drinking heavily to offset the exhaustion. He collapsed and had to make a stay at a sanatorium. Back at work he developed a terror of forgetting his lines, and perhaps of following in his father's uncertain footsteps. Maurice was notorious for not caring to part with an unnecessary sou, but he paid quite a few of them to a personal prompter who sat in the wings and checked every syllable.

Maurice appeared in a new operetta—another huge success— but, again, he collapsed and went back to the sanitorium. His dancing partner from the show, Yvonne Vallée, was at his side. She partnered him in his comeback at the New Empire Theatre in Paris and at the Casino de Paris where he introduced

'Valentine'. The original lyric (it was bowdlerized for the English) contains lines like: 'I took her hand . . . and later everything else.' Hardly morally devastating and, when put over by Maurice Chevalier, unexceptionable. The Spanish Ambassador asked him to sing 'Valentine' in an appearance he was to make before King Alfonso. 'Do you think His Majesty will mind?' asked Maurice. 'It has some things that . . .' 'He'll love it,' said the Ambassador. Maurice began by extolling Valentine's 'little tootsies'—they were all right. In the second eight he came to her little 'tétons' which he loved, so said the song, to 'tâter à tâtons'. The King of Spain, knowing French, was able to appreciate that 'tétons' referred to her tits, which he gathered Maurice enjoyed handling. The king was having a whale of a time but the French Ambassador held his head and rocked as though in pain. Maurice saw the guillotine looming. It transpired that the French Ambassador really was in pain, from a splitting headache.

The year 1927 brought happiness, disaster . . . and tragedy. The happiness was Chevalier's marriage to Yvonne Vallée, the disaster a mere professional one—their appearance together in London in *Whitebirds*. The tragedy was the loss of their child and Yvonne's long convalescence.

Maurice worked alone at the Casino and for the benefit of American tourists sang three songs in English. MGM, in the person of Irving Thalberg, swooped and he was invited to make a screen test. Maurice had appeared in many a silent movie and didn't think his future lay in celluloid. Films, however, did have one relevant attraction: you didn't have to remember your lines for more than a couple of minutes at a time. Maurice agreed, made the test then turned down Thalberg's offer. A good business head is not standard equipment for a genius but Maurice was a match for any. He had insisted the piece of film remain his property. Jesse L. Lasky moved in next, for Paramount. Maurice showed him the MGM test and mentioned that he had turned down Thalberg's offer. Lasky, not knowing what the offer was but knowing he must better it, decided the sky had better be the limit for this unique performer. The sky turned out to be a one-film deal at a huge salary, all expenses paid. If the film was a success he could renegotiate. It may also be a shrewd business move to offer the sky. Maurice accepted. The year was 1928, the month October ... the film, *Innocents of Paris*.

The canny professional in Maurice took no chances with the songs. He included three sure-fire hits from his stage repertoire, one of which—with its cleaned-up English lyric—was 'Valentine'. Leo Robin and Richard Whiting contributed a new song. When Maurice embarked upon it you could feel the cinema public being drawn to this new personality. He wasn't that handsome, he wasn't tall. But the Gallic charm was everything. The smile, the jutting lower lip that was a gift to cartoonists ... the practised jaunty style, the happy assurance that the lady would fall—and not only the lady in the film. Miss Janis, who herself had fallen, had done her work well. Maurice, in performance singing his first screen song 'Louise', was presenting his teacher with a shiny red apple.

Chevalier in Hollywood was an immediate sensation. He was known already to the French-speaking world. From now on the English-speaking, the American-speaking world would be at his feet. For all we know, the Japanese were getting ready to dub him—or sub-title him, since they wouldn't have got round to dubbing. But 'tétons' are universal. The timing of his arrival was perfect. This, in entertainment, is the true meaning of 'luck'. Luck couldn't have made him a star but it put him in Hollywood at a moment when Jolson had established the talking-singing picture and the question on everybody's lips was: 'Where are the stars to follow through, to drive home the success of this barely tried invention?' There was nobody like Chevalier. Whatever the names you may name—and there were quite a few emerging—Maurice Chevalier was at the top of this new tree with the strange foliage. He would stay there for seven triumphant years. The day he was in danger of slipping one branch lower Maurice would quit, on that he was resolved.

For me his most satisfying film performances were in the

movies directed by Ernst Lubitsch. Lubitsch had a brilliant comedy touch and Chevalier was the perfect interpreter. He made four pictures for Lubitsch—the first, in 1929, was *The Love Parade*. He didn't want to make it. A romantic lead? 'I'm over forty,' he said. When somebody told Lubitsch he said, 'In that case he should stop behaving like a twenty-year-old prima donna.' Victor Schertzinger and Clifford Grey wrote the songs. The title piece had Maurice singing that his love reminded him of other loves. 'Charm of Lisette, smile of Mignonette ... the sweetness of Suzette ... in you displayed ...' Only Maurice could have got away with serenading Jeanette MacDonald, of all girls, with the announcement that she was made up of bits and pieces of those gone before. Jeanette was not among the ladies who fell for Maurice. There was, apparently, contact. She described him as 'the fastest derriere pincher in Hollywood'. His view of her was that she lacked humour. On the set—and on the screen, therefore—the professionalism of both gives an illusion of two in harmony. 'Dream lover, put your arms around me ...' sang Jeanette, begging him in song to do all the things she didn't want him to do when they broke for coffee.

With Ernst Lubitsch Maurice was in great womanizing company. Lubitsch was being shown over a house once with a view to his perhaps buying it. The estate agent led him into room after beautiful room. The last was even a film star's dream. 'This,' said the agent, throwing the line away in true Lubitsch fashion, 'is the guest room.' 'My God,' said Lubitsch, aghast, 'she has the best room in the house!'

Maurice took his wife with him to America. They co-starred in a 3-reeler called *Bonjour New York*, shot in the capital but after their arrival in Hollywood she faded into the background, refusing a couple of acting offers that came her way. The press didn't welcome her. They didn't approve of wives, happy marriages making bad stories. They came out in print to the effect that for Maurice to bring her to Hollywood was like taking an old ham sandwich to a banquet. If you don't know the Hollywood score this can be off-putting. Moreover Yvonne was a

The young Maurice (in fact, he was in his 40's) in 1932 with Jeanette MacDonald in *One Hour with You*. Off screen they were not so close.

jealous one, not a thing to be in the big film city where many a derriere is for pinching. Nor should you take your husband too seriously when he is shooting a movie called *The Big Pond* and making love to Claudette Colbert with the sung words 'Living in the sunlight, loving in the moonlight, having a wonderful time!'

When there is a dearth of derrieres the gossip writers will create them. Maurice became involved in a film called *Playboy of Paris* and they made much of the fact that Marlene Dietrich came to visit him on the set. It was a huffy Yvonne who accompanied him on his next trip back to France, and he played the Casino de Paris alone.

'La Louque' was taken ill at this time. She was improving when he sailed for America to film *The Smiling Lieutenant* for Lubitsch in New York but on the first day of shooting Maurice got a cable to say that she had died. He was devastated. After making the trip to Hollywood to film *One Hour With You* for Lubitsch he left with Yvonne for Paris where he would make daily journeys to his mother's grave. Yvonne entered hospital for an operation and was not well enough to sail back to America with him. The gossip writers were quick to make much of her absence and reports soon reached the Paris newspapers that Maurice was dating Miss Dietrich. Yvonne set sail at once. The meeting of the Chevaliers was cool, then acrimonious, and before long downright noisy. Maurice called in his solicitors and—with all-American speed—divorce proceedings were under way. Yvonne behaved courageously and impeccably. When the divorce was made final she refused all offers to publish her story and retired into anonymity. Forty years later she would attend the funeral of Maurice, mourning him with tears.

Maurice spent his new free time reading books. Under the guidance of his friend Charles Boyer he was able to nourish the poor stock of knowledge that scant schooling had managed to instil. He now met his second great director, Rouben Mamoulian. The film was *Love Me Tonight* with music by Richard Rodgers and lyrics by Lorenz Hart. His co-star, again, was the humourless—or derriere-guarding—Jeanette MacDonald.

In 1934 Maurice moved to MGM to make *The Merry Widow*, his fourth and last picture with Lubitsch. Chevalier had reasons for wanting Grace Moore to play the lead but Lubitsch wanted MacDonald, or perhaps Louis B. Mayer wanted Lubitsch to want MacDonald. Whichever way the convolutions turned, I doubt whether even Lubitsch would have coaxed from Miss Moore the delightful high comedy performance Jeanette was able to produce. Up to now we have taken Maurice's success as an actor in our—and his—stride. Comedy is a very tricky form of the business, and high comedy even trickier. Many a good dramatic actor thinks he can step with ease into comedy, only to fall clean through the stage. To say that because you were a passable or even a momentous Lear you can therefore play Coward is as ridiculous as to suggest that Ginger Rogers in her prime would have made a job of Giselle. To me, that this giant of the Café Concert and the Music Hall should be so completely at home treading the trim paths laid out by Lubitsch is a phenomenon for which 'genius' is the only explanation.

Grace Moore having made her name in *One Night of Love* was booked to star in *The Chocolate Soldier*. She asked for Maurice as her co-star but there was one small snag. Miss Moore, having scored one screen success, wanted first billing. Maurice, who had been scoring them for seven years, said 'No' and left Hollywood. It would be twenty-two years before he set foot in the place again. Significantly his last American movie had a French setting. It was called *Folies Bergères*.

In 1940 Lubitsch cabled Maurice to ask him to appear in his satirical *To Be Or Not To Be*. The part went to Jack Benny because France was by then on the verge of collapse and Maurice was about to find himself up to the neck in trouble. The German propaganda machine considered that it would be to their advantage to discredit this national hero and went about it with subtlety. Maurice had a Jewish girl friend named Nita Raya. He had taken her with her parents over the border into what was called 'Free France'. The Gestapo were unable to harm Maurice since martyrdom was at all costs to be avoided but Miss Raya

offered possibilities. Maurice agreed to give a performance at a
prison camp where he had been held during the First War, but
only if they released ten prisoners from districts of his choosing.
An invitation to play in Berlin he refused.

The Gestapo now threatened Nita as a ploy to get Maurice to
appear in Paris. Seeing the beloved Boulevardier living it up on
the stage might, they reasoned, rile the starving Parisians. They
followed this up with an announcement that the French under-
ground movement had killed him for collaborating. It was not
unknown for the German propaganda machine to have more than
one shot, so to speak. We recall that they sank the *Ark Royal*
whenever they were stuck for a success. Having killed off
Maurice they broadcast a statement that he had been beaten to
death by liberationists. The story was carried by newspapers in
this country and in America. Paris was a little surprised, after the
re-taking of Paris, to see him marching in the parade up the
Champs Elysées. Eisenhower's staff had carried out an investiga-
tion and Maurice was cleared of every slander and libel his
detractors had been able to cook up. Nita showed her gratitude
by getting married to a man thirty years younger than Maurice.

He was now able to spend time on his dream: a solo
performance that would draw together all the aspects of his
talent. Songs, many in French ... stories about the songs—he
would need to explain their meanings to English-speaking
audiences, and these explanations formed the most endearing and
brilliantly professional parts of his evening. He opened in New
York at Henry Miller's Theatre in March of 1947 with just a
piano and a minimum of stage props: a cap, a cloak, a pair of
castanets. I shall never forget his desperate efforts to make them
click. He brings them nearer and nearer to his face, quizzing
them ... then, as the curtain falls at the end of the first half, his
nose is caught in them. 'Vingt ans', the song that takes us
through our ever shortening life. The boy of twenty ... he hasn't
a care in the world, says Maurice. Then he reaches thirty ... this
is beautifully acted ... he looks in the mirror and sees one white
hair. And he laughs. He calls his friends in to show them and

they all laugh because, says Maurice, it is very funny to have one white hair. He pulls it out without ceremony and they rock with laughter. Then he is forty and he has many white hairs. He doesn't call anybody. He doesn't do any pulling out either, he'd be bald. The years rush by, he is fifty ... sixty, seventy ... He approaches the long silence. Then the song says—he tells us— that you who are twenty must make the most of it ... love, love, love. Now that we know we are able to sit back and listen, to appreciate the artistry to the full. 'Quai de Bercy' ... His description of the lovers who are broke but may go to the Quai de Bercy to pass a blissful time sniffing at the tubs of wine on the dock. 'Ah, ah, ah!' say the lovers as they sniff. 'Love is the champagne of the poor ...'

Chevalier's communication with his audience is perfectly described by Colette:

Happy the favourite who has built between himself and the public that mysterious, invisible bridge of atoms. On that airy platform he can sing and dance in safety but you may be sure that nothing was left to chance in securing the supreme reward, the hard-won alliance ...

We come to other atoms. The Stockholm Peace Appeal demanded the banning of the atomic bomb by all nations. Many famous folk signed, with the best intent I am sure. I have always held the view that there is something a touch dishonest about using the fame the public has accorded you for other things in order to help promote a political view. Moreover, the artist is a soft touch and the persuader a tough egg. Chevalier's signature was noted by the McCarthy investigators and he was denied further entry to the United States. Not to want a bomb was subversive, they said, or it could be so interpreted. Much damage was done, as we know, to performing careers before McCarthy and company were revealed as being subversive themselves. Or it could be so interpreted.

Maurice was granted a visa in 1955 and made another

triumphant return to Broadway. The McCarthy episode had annulled, perhaps happily, an idea of casting Danny Kaye in a Hollywood-style life story. Maurice was more alive than any of them. Round and round the world he went. In 1957 he was maturely delightful in Billy Wilder's film *Love in the Afternoon*, a performance that led directly to his being cast in *Gigi*. When Maurice introduced his song 'Vingt ans' he used to look up and announce 'When I say twenty years old I can't help looking at the ceiling because that is exactly how old I would like to be.' In *Gigi* he sang 'I'm glad I'm not young any more,' but confessed he didn't quite mean every word of it.

In 1959 he was awarded a special Oscar and it has to be wondered why they waited so long. He said of this occasion:

'I really felt so moved I didn't know how to answer. Afterwards on the plane to Chicago I didn't sleep . . . but not because I couldn't, I didn't want to sleep. I wanted to savour and treasure every moment of that night.'

On his birthday in 1965 somebody asked him how it felt to be seventy-seven. 'Not bad,' he said. 'Considering the alternative.' Then he told how he had achieved his dream but was left with a question mark.

'What keeps me at the top of my line is to be alone on the stage . . . I've got to be satisfied to be Maurice Chevalier and I have been for a very long time . . . but now . . . I must begin to think of the problem of my exit . . . it is the future I have to discuss. It is so important for me to leave the table before I end up under it!'

Patterson Greene, writing in the *Los Angeles Examiner*, said:

Forty-six hundred friendly customers gave Maurice Chevalier a prolonged and resounding welcome when he came upon the stage last night. This was the Chevalier of happily remembered past years, the Chevalier of 'Louise' and 'Valentine'. But, within an hour, the plaudits had reached a second peak and this was even more impressive because it was for the Chevalier today who had substituted warmth, gentleness and occasional wistfulness for the stinging wit and Gallic insouciance of times gone by. It is a change from high summer to mellow autumn . . .

President Eisenhower, who had 'investigated' Maurice in Paris, welcomed him at the White House, and De Gaulle was his host in France.

He filmed in *Can-Can* and—for the first time with his friend Charles Boyer—in *Fanny*. His solo performances continued to take him about the globe until one night, at the Théâtre des Champs Elysées, at the end of a superb evening that had a packed house standing and applauding as though into infinity, he announced: 'You have just seen the last recital I will ever do on a stage anywhere . . .' His problem was solved. He made his exit.

Maurice Chevalier . . . who began at the Café Concert known as the 'Trois Lions' and grew to be a lion in his own right . . . whose touch of genius lay somewhere out on that invisible bridge that has to be made, can only be made by the true artist . . . between artistry and public.

FATS WALLER
The World in his Stride

Thomas 'Fats' Waller – equally at home on organ and piano.

FATS WALLER

The term 'stride' as applied to a certain method of piano playing was first used in the fifties, so Thomas 'Fats' Waller never knew that he was perhaps the greatest ever exponent of it, following in the key-steps of his teacher, James P. Johnson. It means keeping a tremendous beat with the left hand ... striding—playing octaves or single notes or tenths way down and chords up towards the middle ... and letting the right hand float like a chiffon scarf in the wind. Stride is just a basis; it's the style that counts. The touch of stride genius that was the style of Fats Waller was and will be unmistakable.

He was an outsize character ... six feet and something high, three hundred and something pounds heavy, but with a gossamer mind and a heart as big as the Savoy Ballroom. Some with smaller cardiac capacities would damage, sadden and bewilder him. Others—the wide public, for instance—would glory in the magnanimity of his talent.

Thomas Waller, pianist, composer of great standard melodies and vocalist extraordinary, was one of eleven children, only five of whom survived past childhood. He was born in Harlem, New York, on May 21st 1904. His father, Edward Waller, was in the trucking business—in a small way: horses pulled trucks at the turn of the century. His mother, Adeline, was in the business of keeping Edward, their children and herself alive, which in America at that time was not too easy if you were poor, and especially not if you were what was then called 'coloured'.

Edward and Adeline Waller were pillars of the Abyssinian

Baptist Church, so the Waller children had to watch their step. Right from diaper days young Thomas Waller had a giant share of charm, which he used more and more as he grew up—and out. No one in the family except his father Edward was proof against it. The very birds in the trees surrendered and later other birds, too, would fall. This same charm would embrace his audiences, and the watching and listening world would open its arms to him. Did I say he grew up? I don't think he ever did that. It was perhaps the secret of his appeal and the reason he was so rarely out of trouble. But it gave him a personality you could warm your hands at.

When you are a devout Baptist and trucking hard all week it isn't unnatural that you should truck on down to God at the week end. Edward and Adeline Waller were leading kindly lights of street corner prayer meetings. Thomas Waller, aged six, played on the harmonium notes he'd picked up from his mother then, back at home, he would climb one floor to have a go at the piano upstairs. His brother Bob later caught him downstairs playing on two chairs for a keyboard. This—and the fact that Thomas Waller rolled sad eyes—touched him to the point of pushing hard for a Waller piano, which a relative at last supplied. Father paid a Miss Perry to give them all lessons.

There was by now a final baby in the Waller family, christened Edith. Thomas sat her on the piano stool and twiddled her round. When he got up speed she shot across the room. 'Not me!' cried older sister Naomi, who was built like a brick house and known as 'Little Jack Johnson', 'it was Thomas!' Mrs Waller picked up baby Edith, and then a leather strap. Thomas, knowing mother was a sucker for the religious approach, said, 'The devil made me do it, Mom ...' Mrs Waller hesitated, the punitive strap already in mid-air, while Thomas rolled wide eyes between the strap and her. 'Mom ...' he said. 'Don't you think we should pray?' Pray they did. Prayers don't make the bottom sore, the boy no doubt reasoned. Just the knees.

Thomas studied music at school too. He played the organ for the kids as they filed into and out of assembly. Thomas gave it a beat which delighted them. He also made faces at them which delighted them more. The only comment in his school report, however, was that Thomas Waller was now pianist in the school orchestra. His proud father took him to Carnegie Hall to hear Paderewski, and Thomas was enormously impressed. God, of course, knew where all this was going to lead. Edward Waller thought it would lead to the classics, but he wasn't omniscient.

Adeline Waller liked to cook—which was just as well because who else was going to do it?—and Thomas loved eating. One day a school chum came to the door and asked 'Is Fats at home?' Mother didn't like it but big sister Naomi did, and wouldn't let it rest. 'Fats' she insisted he became—for one thing it took some of the attention off her own girth.

Adeline Waller's health began to fail. They moved to an apartment with fewer stairs, and responsibility set in. Naomi was now running the household and Fats took an after-school job delivering groceries for seventy-five cents a week. A gang of white youths cornered him and went for him, leaving him with a knife wound and a lasting impression. To a lyric that said 'What did I do to be so black and blue?' he would one day write a deeply felt melody.

Today there is nothing untoward about singing a hymn in pop style in church. In the twenties such ragging around would have been considered blasphemy. One day Fats was seated at the church organ playing a hymn. The church was empty, he thought. When he got to the second chorus—or verse, I suppose, since it was a hymn—he gave it ever such a slight beat. Then a less slight one. Then, it had to be confessed, he was swinging. His father announced his presence at this point and Fats was lucky not to swing from the church rafters. As Shakespeare has it: 'No place indeed should murder sanctuarize', and murder, in Edward's view, was the crime his delinquent son had committed. He settled for dragging the boy home to meet a different beat.

Edward Waller disapproved of any music that wasn't classical or sacred. By now he was becoming uneasy and made a harsh decision. If Fats wanted to continue with his music studies he would have to leave school and work at a full-time job so that he could pay for his own lessons. Father got him the job, with his sister Naomi, in a downtown factory that made jewel boxes. It was a boring job, making jewel boxes for somebody else's jewels. In the lunch hour a certain pastor's son showed a certain fat fifteen-year-old how to squeeze through the basement window at the local church. The last bit needed a push, he would certainly never have made it alone. Organs are loudish but the church had a piano, which, the neighbours discovered, had a plump ghost that played during the lunch break. The ghost was enjoying it so much he went on playing after the lunch break and got the sack. Fats became a delivery boy again, which gave him more time for practice. It may have given him a taste for liquor, though we can't be sure. Prohibition was going strong, and Fats' deliveries included rot-gut whisky and bath-tub gin.

Father and son continued to argue about this thing called 'jazz'. 'The devil's music' was anathema to the Abyssinian Baptist mind of Edward Waller. More correctly, he didn't understand it, was frightened of it and didn't want to take chances in case somebody up there wasn't too sure about him. He had the religious man's absolute knowledge of what God likes and what He doesn't. He knew, for instance, that God hated the movies. Fats knew he knew God hated the movies. Fats didn't mind too much about the movies, but the music that went with them was something quite different. They showed movies at the Lincoln Theatre in Harlem, and had music—an organ, a piano ... It was the devil's house, but young Thomas, with Faustian disregard, paid his soul at the box office.

Mazie Mullins made the piano keyboard talk at the Lincoln and Fats drank in every note. She wondered who this lad was, in the front row day after day and bulging out of his clothes, especially out of his short trousers. She befriended him and before long had him sitting in the pit next to her as she played. Fats who had charmed the leather strap out of his mother's hand now charmed Mazie off her piano stool. 'You don't want to tire yourself, Miss Mullins,' he said. 'You should take a break ...'

She did take a break. And Fats actually played the piano while Mazie went out for a minute. The organ was the next step, or stop. One day when the relief organist fell ill Fats' latest charmee, the lady who ran the Lincoln Theatre, asked him to take over. She paid him.

Fats was equally at home on all keyboards—later he would swing, charmingly, on a celeste. At the organ of the Lincoln he was in his element. He wasn't playing hymns so a touch of swing was permissible. His school pals got the word and came in droves to egg him on. 'Make it rock, Fats!' they yelled. He did. Fats hammed it up both facially and on the keyboards, and the audience, kids and grown-ups alike, were swept along by the sheer joy that emanated from this rough-playing, bottom-bouncing, eye-rolling, happy lad with a solid beat that would have knocked nails well into the coffin of any church-going objector. Fats was a huge success at the Lincoln. He was moving out of the hooch business and into—what? The devil's business? If that's what bringing a smile to people's faces and lifting them out of the doldrums means, then Thomas Waller was in it up to the neck. His fame spread over Harlem and Father Edward came to know that his son had talent. He never went to the devil's house to hear him, and Mother was either not well enough or was not encouraged to go alone.

Young Thomas was engaged to play at a local party in the open air and met Edith Hatchett. We have to wonder what she was doing there, since she was corseted in religion. The Waller parents were happy to accept her (that should have been a red light to Fats) and the pressure was on. Here was an angel, thought the Wallers, sent from Heaven to save Thomas from his plump and erring self. Miss Hatchett would later do her utmost to chop Fatsie into pieces. Some would think he deserved it.

Edith Hatchett wanted her prospect to learn a trade. Thomas 'Fats' Waller, it was her considered opinion, should give up music. A real angel stepped in and his job at the Lincoln became a permanent one. Twenty-three dollars a week would be enough to quieten even an Abyssinian Baptist, you might think. But religious difference, not for the first or last time, brought tragedy. The rows grew fiercer at home, and the louder voice was his father's. Adeline could stand the strain no longer; she had a stroke and died at the age of forty-eight. The year was 1920. Fats was desolate. Twenty years later he would burst into tears while playing 'Sometimes I feel like a motherless child' and refuse to complete the recording.

Fats Waller was desperate to improve his technique. During a Harlem gig in a tent he approached Russell Brooks, a popular local pianist and a friend, at the piano and tried to charm lessons out of him. Russell was no teacher but promised to introduce the lad to James P. Johnson who was the idol of Harlem. Fats was so excited that he made a whooping exit, caught his feet in the guy ropes and brought down the tent. It put paid to the introduction. Fats left home and parked himself at the Brooks' house—Russell had married and moved out. The Brooks had a player piano and Fats would put on a James P. Johnson roll and stop and re-start it, fitting his fingers into the chords. Russell came in one day and caught him at it. He remembered the promise he had made the night the tent came down and the delayed meeting with the great James P. followed. The Johnsons took Fats under their wing, Mrs Johnson endeared herself to him for ever by buying him his first long pants.

Fats began a daily routine. His mornings were taken up with fitting his fingers into piano roll chords, his afternoons playing at the Lincoln, his evenings learning from James P. Johnson and his late nights at Le Roys, a famous Harlem music spot. His next stop would be the 'rent parties'. These were thrown by impecunious apartment dwellers trying not to get evicted. They would engage one or two pianists at a few dollars a time, cook up a little food then charge admission. The proceeds would find their way into the landlord's pocket—with, it was hoped and prayed, a little something over. A feature of the rent party was the 'cutting session'. One pianist would give his all, then be 'cut' by another, perhaps unpaid and there just for a drink and the hell of it. He would find his predecessor had left him in a particularly uninviting key, such as A major. He, in turn, would leave his successor in F sharp, saying, 'Take it out o' that,' as he surrendered the piano chair. There were white visitors eager to learn—the young George Gershwin, for one, picked up his own stride style at the rent parties.

The parties would go on all night and encroach on the morrow—or the morrows, some continued throughout the weekend. They were marvellous for the piano techniques but hazardous, to put it lightly, for the health. Great jazz musicians tend not to be good insurance risks. The paid pianists at the rent parties got their food for nothing, as much as they could eat. Fats was unpaid as yet but, in any case, alcohol was fast becoming food and drink to him, and the liquor flowed freely.

Edith Hatchett bided her time. Fats was a lonely seventeen-year-old when she said a few words of kindness that reminded him of his mother. He proposed and was accepted. They married and moved in with the religious Hatchetts. Not one of them approved, including the Hatchett who was now 'Waller', when Fats went off on tour with 'Liza and her Shufflin' Six'. Fats met Bill (soon to be 'Count') Basie in Boston and later gave him lessons at the Lincoln. The Hatchetts didn't think much of Basie, indeed, it isn't easy to be clear what they did think much of on weekdays.

Edith became pregnant and Fats was warned that babies eat money. He pushed hard and got his first paid rent-party booking and was a smash hit. But not with Edith. The trouble was that she and Fats had each a mistaken idea about the other. Edith was sure he would give up music and settle down, Fats was sure that if he got more and more music to play and could settle up all would be well. It never was. Thomas Waller Junior was born in the spring of 1922. Thomas Senior was eighteen years old. He went on tour to make some scratch and when he returned was confronted by the two older Hatchetts and one Waller with a second squealing Waller in her arms. Fats, they demanded, must take up a trade. They had one earmarked for him—carpentry. Fats didn't bother using his charm. He said 'No' to woodwork and that, virtually, was the end of the marriage.

Fats had begun composing. In Boston, or perhaps when leaving Boston to go Hatchettwards, he wrote a piece which he called 'Boston blues'. Now he turned to composition for solace. The Lincoln was bought up to be used for movies only and the new owners had also acquired the bigger Lafayette Theatre. Fats went in at fifty dollars a week, playing the first grand organ in Harlem. He now met Clarence Williams who had started a publishing company. Williams wanted to publish his compositions but Fats wasn't keen—he hadn't bothered to write them down. Williams arranged for him to record for Okeh Records as an accompanist. Again, Fats wasn't interested but Williams talked him into it. The only snag was that Fats didn't turn up for the session. Another was arranged but again, no Fats. Most fixers would have given up at this point but Clarence Williams persevered. He tried to get Fats' life into some sort of order, even trying to patch up the marriage. Here, luckily, he had no luck; it never could have worked. But at the third try he did get Fats to the recording studio and within two months he had made eight sides. He began to make piano rolls ... somewhere, perhaps, some Harlem kid would one day be fitting his fingers into the Waller chords. The next move for Williams was to persuade Fats to put his compositions on to paper for publication. Clarence Williams supplied the lyrics and in five years they wrote more than seventy songs. Not one was memorable.

Fats entered a piano contest and won, playing 'Carolina shout' composed by his former teacher, James P. Johnson. After the concert a man about ten years his senior introduced himself. By an extraordinary coincidence his mother's maiden name had been 'Waller'. His father had been the Madagascarian Consul to the United States and his name was Andrea Menentania Razafinkeriefo. Nobody could say it, so he changed it to Andy Razaf. Waller and Razaf would have no difficulty in turning out memorable pieces, like 'Ain't misbehavin''. Fats, who had married at seventeen, was divorced at nineteen and Edith Waller, née Hatchett, and their offspring had to be supported. Fats begins one recording of the song with the spoken words: 'This is to tell you that I've paid my alimony and I ain't misbehavin' . . .' It wasn't, alas, always forthcoming—not with regularity.

Fats and Andy Razaf made the rounds of the publishers. These gentlemen, in those early days of copyright, paid an advance but were not noted for coughing up the royalties due. What's crooked for the goose, the writers may have thought . . . They countered by selling a song for a twenty-five, or sometimes fifty dollar advance, then popping round the corner to another firm and selling it again. And again and again. The publishers didn't mind too much, since at that time it was not a matter of who bought a song but who published it first, thereby establishing a copyright.

Alimony was a nightmare to Fats. He forgot it, spent the money, remembered it . . . then forgot it again, finally landing up in jail. Williams and Razaf and two other friends dug up five hundred dollars bail and arrived to find Fats living it up in a cell with a millionaire. 'Save your money,' said Fats to them, 'it's great in here!' The millionaire, who had chosen to be incarcerated rather than pay what he called 'blood money' to his wife, was providing food and booze, even a piano. The three things Fats wanted from life, or rather three of the four. The friends retired and Fats, remembering the fourth necessity of life, charmed his bail out of the millionaire.

Prohibition, like a bad marriage, had come to an end and the gangsters moved into the brothel circuit. The famous one was immortalized by Count Basie in his 'Swingin' at the Daisy Chain'. Fats was a frequent visitor there, playing the piano with a bottle of Scotch and a few ladies in attendance. The madame of the Daisy Chain was Hazel Valentine, who herself was immortalized by Fats in 'Valentine stomp'.

Fats had an apartment in Harlem where he lived beyond his alimonial means. A certain Captain Maines was now helping. He had heard Fats play in Harlem and got him bookings on what was called 'the upper crust circuit'. Downtown socialite parties were enlivened by Bill 'Bojangles' Robinson, for example, with Fats at the piano. Around the corner from Fats' Harlem pad was Mother

An early Victor catalogue in which Thomas Waller of Harlem makes his first appearance.

Shepherd's, a combined boarding house, barber shop, snack counter and grocery. Fats became a frequent visitor ... he was fascinated by the grand-daughter of the house, sixteen-year-old Anita Rutherford. She came to the Lafayette and Fats played just for her. He tried to date her but she insisted he meet Mother and Father first. Fats proposed and she asked for time to think it over. She checked with Captain Maines who told her that Fats had a great future if she could straighten him out, and he thought she could. When Maines told Fats that Anita loved him but didn't want a mess for a husband, Fats crossed his heart this would be for keeps and meant it. He and Anita were married in 1926.

Fats began applying himself to work, writing for shows, playing, recording. He recorded on the Columbia label with the Fletcher Henderson band and toured the campuses with them. He made his first solo recording for Victor on their church organ in New Jersey and accompanied Alberta Hunter for the same company. They insisted on labelling him 'Thomas Waller'.

Maurice Thomas Waller was born on September 10th 1927, when his father was twenty-three, and these three Wallers seemed to have a secure future ahead of them. Captain Maines, manager, family friend and financial watch dog, fixed Fats with Louis Armstrong at the Vendome Theatre in Chicago. Anita, unlike his first wife, the reluctant Edith, went along, taking Maurice. Anita Waller became pregnant again and it was happiness all round. But ... the watch-dog must have nodded. Fats had, certainly. He had forgotten his alimony. Edith had him arrested and three Wallers trekked back to New York where a sympathetic judge let him off with a caution. Fats breathed again, but not for long; he defaulted once more and this time it was jail. Sadly, his father died while he was behind bars.

It was Gene Austin the singer who pleaded for his release. The judge was in a sour mood. 'Is there a good reason ...' he asked, 'why I should free this man?' 'I need him for a recording this afternoon,' Gene improvised. The judge had no ear for music, 'So what?' he snapped. Gene may have picked up a little of the

Waller charm technique. 'If he doesn't play,' he said, 'it'll put men out of work and these are hard times, your Honour.' Fats got off with a lecture but he had to agree that all future alimony payments be made into court. He did have a job, anyway—that afternoon, Gene told him, following through. He took Fats to the studio but the other musicians, being white, refused to play with him. The matter was solved by putting Fats in a corner with his own microphone and a screen. Fats was full of love for all mankind but it's a wonder his heart didn't harden like a rock that day.

The birth of Ronald Waller in November 1928 meant that twenty-four-year-old Fats had to knuckle down even harder. The Immerman brothers, who owned Connie's Inn in Harlem, engaged him and Andy Razaf to write songs for their new show *Hot Chocolates*. Luckily, Andy was a touch more on the ball than Fats. He pushed him into a taxi, took him to his mother's house and sat him down at the piano. In two hours they had two songs. Fats was thirsty and thought this called for a celebration, but Andy pressed him to sit down again and write one more, a soft-shoe number, such as every show had to have. The music was all but completed when Mr Waller, like Dickens' Mr Weller, took his hat and his leave. Andy continued writing then had to telephone all over town to find the melody writer. 'It's finished,' he said. 'What is?' Fats asked. He'd forgotten the melody but Andy Razaf had a better memory, except for the bridge, the middle bit. He sang the rest to Fats over the 'phone and luckily it rang a bell. Fats hummed a middle eight and they had one of their biggest world successes, 'Honeysuckle rose'.

Connie's *Hot Chocolates* was a smash hit and made the names of Cab Calloway and James Baskette who would be Uncle Remus in Walt Disney's *Song of the South*. The show moved down town with two added numbers, 'Black and blue' and 'Ain't misbeha-vin'', sung by Louis Armstrong. To misbehave or not to misbehave . . . like Hamlet, Fats had his problems. He couldn't help womanizing. It didn't mean anything but wives don't like it. Anita tried to be understanding. With one flirtation after another she was prepared to cope and it was only when Fats was attentive to one girl for too long that she took a plane to sort out the situation.

Ex-wife Edith had been doing sums. *Hot Chocolates* being a downtown success too, she decided she wanted a bigger piece of the improved action. This threw Fats into a panic he would regret all his life. He sold his royalties in the *Hot Chocolates* songs (there were twenty in all) for five hundred dollars. He would collect no more on 'Ain't Misbehavin''. Nor, incidentally, would his ex-wife, but she wouldn't have appreciated the point. It was work-till-you-drop time for Fats. Luckily the jobs came in, and radio proved to be a great medium for him. Up to now Andy Razaf had sung their songs to publishers, since he couldn't persuade Fats to open his mouth. Now, on radio, it seemed the only way to project his personality, and his singing style quickly became a sensation.

Phil Ponce had taken over as Fats' manager and the work pressure began to mount. Touring brought its rewards, but also its sadnesses when he was refused admission to hotels and restaurants. It seemed he was not wanted for his colour, yet was in high demand for his talent. RKO paid him five thousand dollars for a one-day appearance in the film *Hooray for Love*, Anita accompanying him to Hollywood.

The Waller work schedule was staggering. On his return to New York he recorded forty-four songs in two full days at the studio. Five days later he recorded thirty in one day, then was back on the road. Hollywood again, to make *King of Burlesque*. The whole of 1936 was spent touring, often playing a different town every night. His contract at the Apollo Theatre in Harlem called for two appearances a day. Oddly, it was the health of his manager, Phil Ponce, that gave under the strain. Ed Kirkeby took over from Ponce and arranged more tours. The racial difficulties began to get Fats down. The tyres on his car were slashed, sand was poured in the engine; finally Kirkeby decided he should leave the country for a spell, and arranged a ten-week tour of Britain and Scandinavia.

When I was in Hollywood at the beginning of 1938 I saw that Fats was billed as appearing at a Variety Theatre in downtown Los Angeles. I raced to buy a seat, and after the performance I raced backstage. Fats had been my idol since I had heard him for the first time on one of the first auto-change gramophones. When I told him so the eyebrows went up, the eyes opened wide, he enclosed my hand in a massive, welcoming fist ... I shall never forget the warmth and hugeness of his laughter. At the end of the week I left for England on a freighter. The trip took five weeks, and I arrived full of the news that I had actually seen and met Fats Waller. The wind was taken completely out of my sails when I learned that he was topping the bill at the London Palladium.

Time, that old hustler, was running out fast. Touring America in one-night stands was now like mountaineering to Fats. He began to lose his appetite. He was by nature an enormous eater though he did seem to eat in shifts. He'd play the piano all night long to whoever would listen, always with a bottle to imbibe from. This would take his mind off the fleshpots. Then, all of a sudden, he would feel the need to eat, and polish off twenty-seven pork chops (his son Maurice gave me this strange figure). He would take an hour or more to do it, returning again and again to the platter, refilled not only with pork chops but with potatoes and anything else that was going. Having demolished all, he would attack and clean an enormous dish of pie that would have fed the family for a week.

By now Fats was down to a dozen pork chops. He was always catching colds. 'Cut out the liquor and the late hours,' said the doctor, which is like telling a bus conductor to keep away from tickets. He did do something about the liquor. Instead of whisky he ordered white wine—but two truckloads of it. He would have been better sticking to half a truck of malt. He did have one break in touring but Kirkeby, his manager, who no doubt was on a percentage filled it for him with a film appearance in *Stormy Weather*.

Fats began his last tour. Everywhere he met the same racial opposition. The head waiter, who had perhaps joined in giving him an ovation at the theatre, wouldn't allow him to enter the dining room. He rang for room service and nothing happened. The other side of this tarnished coin is that, because he was constantly travelling out of working hours to give shows to the Forces, a train that would not normally stop in Omaha did halt to pick him up at the order of the commander of the troops he had entertained.

His last appearance was at the Zanzibar Room in Hollywood. The air conditioning blew ice cold air on to him as he sat at the piano but he made no complaint. His resistance sapped by overwork and over-indulgence, he collapsed with 'flu and developed a lung infection. He refused to go to hospital and spent ten days in his hotel room, where this time we assume he was allowed some service. He was on the stand again at the Zanzibar at the end of this short gap and continued working at full pitch to finish the engagement. He attended a press party before getting on the train for Chicago and New York—he so looked forward to the rest the journey would give him. He was drinking heavily, either to help him through the chores or perhaps because he sensed that he was past repair.

The train crossed the Kansas plains in a blizzard. Fats slept the first night and all next day. It was during the second night he died. Ed Kirkeby found him in his sleeper berth next morning as the train was pulling into Kansas City. The date was December 15th 1943. Fats was thirty-nine. Another train was waiting at a siding, and one of the passengers on it was Louis Armstrong. 'What's going on over there?' he asked a guard. 'They say Fats Waller is on board and just died.' Satchmo burst into tears.

During his short lifetime Fats wrote hundreds of melodies and swing pieces, many of which are still coming to light. The great ones we know are 'Honeysuckle rose', 'Ain't Misbehavin'', 'Keepin' out of mischief now' (two songs with a single lyrical thought), 'I've got a feeling I'm falling'... There are others (I could name at least one giant standard, but I won't) claimed by other composers. They are among the manuscript ideas Fats sold for a few dollars when he needed alcohol or alimony. Sometimes when you hear a familiar tune and can't put a name to it—it could be Waller's 'Handful of keys', 'Yacht club swing', 'Viper's drag' ... These are more easily identifiable when played by Fats himself, or by the distinctive group sound of 'Fats Waller and his Rhythm'. The makers of the sound usually included Gene 'Honeybear' Cedric on clarinet and tenor sax, Cedric Wallace string bass, Herman Autry trumpet and the young Al Casey, who brought along his guitar in 1933 at the age of eighteen and stayed the course.

Fats had been thinking it was time he wrote a melodic piece. One night he arrived home, in the small hours as ever, and tore up the stairs calling to his sleeping wife. Anita said, 'Don't shout, you'll wake Maurice.' 'Wake him!' said Fats. 'Get him down. I just wrote something that's as good as Gershwin!' He went to the organ he had had installed and played the graceful—and strangely named—'Jitterbug waltz'.

Many are the songs Fats recorded that are not, in fact, his compositions. He made them so much his own they will always be associated with him. It tells you something, I think, about the man that the most successful of these are the simplest, the most innocent, the most romantic ... 'I'm gonna sit right down and write myself a letter', 'When somebody thinks you're wonderful' ... 'My very good friend the milkman ... says that I've been losing too much sleep ... He doesn't like the hours I keep and he suggests that I should marry you'. It was a pity that milkman didn't come home before the milk and suggest Fats marry Anita first. He adored her in his fashion. Maurice Waller told me that some time after his father's death he asked his young, attractive mother why she had never remarried. Her reply was that she didn't want to lose the name of Waller.

We all have our favourite aspect of Thomas Waller. He was a great clown, a marvellous composer, a great stride player, perhaps the greatest ... Personally, I remember the gentler Fats ... the Fats who sang 'A little bit independent', and:

I KNOW WHY EACH HONEY BEE
HAS TO FEEL JEALOUS OF ME ...

THEY SEARCH BY THE HOUR
UNTIL THEY ARE BLUE . . .
THEY CAN'T FIND A FLOWER
AS LOVELY AS YOU . . . NO, NO, BABY . . .

For all his 300 pounds he was a gentle man.

Thomas Fats Waller . . . If one had used in his presence the cliché 'It's a great life if you don't weaken', he would probably have said, 'Man . . . it's a whole lot greater if you do,' adding, perhaps, his gorgeous phrase: 'One never knows, do one . . .?'

FRED ASTAIRE
After You, Who?

My earliest memory of Fred Astaire is on stage in *The Gay Divorce* in 1933. He looked like this.

FRED ASTAIRE

'His sister Adele has the real talent,' said their father. 'And maybe Fred will come around to it one day too . . .' Brother and sister Astaire were born Fred and Adele Austerlitz but were not to stay that way for long. Herr Austerlitz Sr travelled from Austria to the New World in 1895 and settled in Omaha, Nebraska. Coming from a longish line of brewers he went, not unnaturally, into beer. But he was a lover of music and of the theatre, and so too was the American lady he married while she was still in her teens. Adele Austerlitz was born in 1897 and Fred came along eighteen months later, on May 10th 1899. Adele, with the 'real talent', attended dancing school and Fred went along for the ride. 'Dancing was something my sister did,' he observed later. Said Adele: 'He tried his best.'

Fred's best couldn't have been that bad. When Fred was five years old father sent mother and the kids off to New York to seek their professional dancing fortune. Money was scarce but they managed, father working hard at home and having faith. It was decided that 'Austerlitz' wouldn't, so to speak, fit the bill. It didn't fit too well in Omaha, Nebraska, so Austerlitz borrowed one of their grandmothers' names and they all became 'Astaire'.

Fred and Adele did well at Claude Alvienne's school in New York, both in dance and in drama. Fred even appeared in a school production of *Cyrano de Bergerac* as Roxane, opposite Adele's Cyrano, the excuse being that she was three inches taller. She may even have had a longer nose. Their young mother (she was now in her early twenties) taught them reading, writing and arithmetic at home and also, as a wise mother and a theatre lover, took them to see the great performers of the day. They saw the Danish ballerina Adeline Genée eight times in *The Soul Kiss*. According to Fred, 'Mother hoped some of Genée's dancing would rub off on us.'

Professor Alvienne who ran the school devised an act for the Astaires. It involved a huge wedding cake, one you could dance upon, if you were rising no age at all. Adele played the bride, Fred the groom wearing, for the very first time, a top hat. After the dance the cake lit up and each Astaire in turn did a solo. Fred came back as a lobster, Adele as a glass of champagne. There was more dancing and some playing of musical bells with hands and feet. I don't think this act would have appealed to me personally, but with the American public the Astaires were a sensation. They opened as professionals at Keyport, New Jersey—Fred was six, Adele seven. The man in the paper said: 'The Astaires are the greatest child act in Vaudeville.' Fred, when grown up, added, 'In Keyport.' At this point a gentleman named Elbridge T ▬ nas Gerry stepped in to champion all stage children against all stage-parental comers. Soon the law set an age limit—at between fourteen and sixteen—so that young children in Vaudeville had to give up their work or act up their ages. Fred stepped early into long trousers and got taken for a bell-top.

The young Astaires paused at this awkward age and went to a real school for two years. Then it was on to Ned Wayburn's dancing school in New York. Mother Astaire paid Ned Wayburn $1,000, a huge sum at that time, to arrange a new act. Up to now Adele had drawn the notices, even the bookers' reports. One had read: 'The girl seems to have talent but the boy can do nothing.' Nevertheless, in the spirit of the Kern and Fields song he would sing later, Fred picked himself up, dusted himself off ... and prepared to start all over again.

'We played,' said Fred, 'every rat trap and chicken coop in the Middle West for two years. We did pretty well in Pawtucket but died the death of a dog in Woonsocket.' They suffered much from having to be the first act on the bill. The audience either

hadn't arrived or were shuffling into their seats. 'First on' is the
most vulnerable of spots, in which it is difficult not to die the
death of a dog. If you do there's nowhere lower they can move
you. Once they were actually replaced by a dog act, but we don't
know whether it died the death of a man ... At last they got to
follow something: a newsreel. This meant, at least, that most of
the patrons were in their seats by the time the Astaires took the
stage. They took it by storm. The manager moved them to
Number Three, where they stopped the show and had to come
down from their dressing rooms to take another curtain call.
They passed Eddie Cantor, waiting to make his entrance. 'What
is this,' he said, 'the Gans–Nelson fight?' (I don't know who they
were either but it doesn't matter.)

Back in New York they called in at the publishers to hear new
songs. These were demonstrated at the piano by song pluggers.
One of them heard Fred say he'd like to get into musical comedy.
'Wouldn't it be great', the plugger said, 'if I could write one and
you could be in it.' 'Who are you?' Fred asked. 'Gershwin.
George Gershwin.'

Fred was seventeen when he took a full page ad in *Variety*, the
performers' weekly. The result was a contract for a musical
show—no more Vaudeville, this was a revue. Lee and J. J.
Shubert presented it at their new roof-top show place above the
44th Street Theatre. The apt title was *Over the Top*. It was a
success and the critics went for the Astaires, in the nicer sense.
'One of the prettiest features of the show,' they said, 'is the
dancing of the two Astaires. The girl, a light, sprite-like little
creature, has really an exquisite floating style in her caperings,
while the young man combines eccentric agility with humor.'

After the New York run the Shuberts followed the usual
practice and took the show on the road. In Washington the
Astaires were seen by Charles Dillingham who signed them up.
They had to play in another revue for the Shuberts first—*The
Passing Show of 1918*.

Fred Astaire was to mention later that luck didn't come much
into things. 'We had to saw our way through,' he said, and

anyone who knows anything about entertainment in any form from the inside will be completely at one with the phrase. However, he now had one piece of luck many a lad could have done with. He reached the draft age just after the end of the war in Europe. The revue *The Passing Show of 1918* had a throw-away advertisement that was typical of the day. It read:

IT'S A WHALE—WITHOUT JONAH!
A HUGE WHIZZING ENTERTAINMENT!
A BRILLIANT ARRAY OF TALENT WITH THE WINTER GARDEN'S
  FAMOUS WIGGLING WAVE OF WINSOME WITCHES!!!
150 PEOPLE . . . 2 ACTS . . . 25 SCENES . . .

The bit about the 'wiggling witches' may have been written by one of the Shuberts. They were a successful pair but some thought them short on style. There is a story that at the Shubert Theatre in Chicago a frustrated fellow—whether an actor, director, stage manager or whatever, who knows?—had jotted on the wall of the men's room 'YOU ARE THE ONLY MAN IN THIS THEATRE WHO KNOWS WHAT HE'S DOING'.

The Astaires began rehearsing *Apple Blossoms* for Charles Dillingham. Fritz Kreisler, who had composed some of the music, was present and played the piano while Fred and Adele went through a dance routine. Fred, having been brought up in proper awe of the great, was impressed enough at having Kreisler as his rehearsal pianist. On another occasion they heard George Gershwin's voice. 'Hey, Freddie!' he called out from the pit where he was playing a rehearsal stint, 'We'll be doing that show together yet!'

Apple Blossoms was an operetta. The Astaires did no speaking but had just two dancing appearances, scoring a huge success within a success. Alexander Woolcott wrote about them in the *New York Times*, mis-spelling their names, a carelessness that always infuriates an artist. In this case it might have been the fault of the man who set up the type. I think it was Woolcott's.

'There should be,' he wrote, 'half a dozen special words for the vastly entertaining dances by the two Adaires—in particular for those by the incredibly nimble and lackadaisical Adaire named Fred . . .' He had finally overtaken Adele Adaire, anyway! 'He,' continued Woolcott, '. . . is one of those extraordinary persons whose sense of rhythm and humor have been all mixed up, whose very muscles—of which he seems to have an extra supply—are downright facetious . . .'

Charles B. Dillingham—'C.B.', as he was called by intimates—adored the Astaires and they him. At Christmas a small package with a cheque arrived. 'Dear Freddie,' the note said, 'I am sending you and Adele a little Christmas present. Sister can have the ring and you can get yourself just what you want. Thanking you for being such a success in *Apple Blossoms* . . .' Such employers did exist. I don't think they do any more.

Apple Blossoms fell and C.B. presented the Astaires in *The Love Letter*, another operetta but not another hit. The memorable matter about it is that Teddy Royce choreographed what was to be an Astaire trade mark. Royce got Adele Astaire to put out her arms as though she were riding a bicycle. 'Now run round the stage in a large circle as if you are very intent on getting somewhere,' he said, and demonstrated for her—singing 'Oompah, oompah, oompah' as he went. 'Now,' he said to Fred, 'You join Adele, shoulder to shoulder, doing the same . . . After three or four run-arounds make an exit. The audience will go mad for encores, you'll see.' He set Adele in motion and demonstrated for Fred, this time shouting to the pianist 'Play a lot of ooompahs!' The run-around became known as the 'Oompah Trot'. They used it in five shows. 'You need a nutty song for it,' Royce had said. It was a riot but it didn't save *The Love Letter*.

A young manager named Alex Aarons dispelled the gloom for the Astaires with the news that he had a show for them called *For Goodness' Sake*. The critics dispelled more gloom when it opened in New York in February of 1922, and was a great success. It travelled to London with a new title, *Stop Flirting*, opening on

May 30th 1923 at the Shaftesbury Theatre—the original Shaftesbury, across the road from the side of the Palace Theatre. It is a
car park today. The Astaires conquered London. 'When we
made our exit,' said Fred, 'the roof came down.' The Germans,
of course, literally brought it down later. The nutty run-around
song in *Stop Flirting* was 'The whichness of the whatness of the
whereness of the who'.

Fred and Adele now began an oompah trot of the social stage.
The Royals came in force to see them. The Prince of Wales, the
Duke and Duchess of York, later to be King and Queen ...
Prince George, later the Duke of Kent ... The Astaires went
night clubbing, racing. Fred acquired a wardrobe from the
world's finest tailors, in Savile Row, and the manner of wearing
them that never left him. His clothes were to be a byword of
beauty, just as those of Ginger Rogers would be another kind of
byword. Mrs Astaire joined them in London but Papa, who had
seen and rejoiced in *For Goodness' Sake* in New York, stayed
firmly at home. He would never accept that a father should do
any other thing than provide for his family. If they didn't need
such provision they should not provide for him. Work he would,
and that was the end of it.

After a few months *Stop Flirting* moved down Shaftesbury
Avenue to the Queen's—strangely, another theatre the Germans
were later to bomb. It was at the Queen's that the Prince of Wales
saw the show. When Adele heard he was in front she said, 'Well,
good ... What kept him?' The Prince came again some nights
later and entertained Fred and Adele at the Riviera Club. There
he asked Adele 'Are you too tired to dance with me?' 'Sir,' she
answered, 'I'm exhausted.' With which, she jumped up and
rushed at him.

They moved again, to the Strand Theatre, then moved out to
be replaced by the usual pantomime. Over Christmas they played
for five weeks in Birmingham. A three-week vacation in Paris
followed, then it was back to the Strand Theatre and the glorious
perks of success. One of the non-perks is that personal matters
often must go by the board. Mrs Astaire had returned to America

to nurse a sick husband. She cabled Sir Alfred Butt, the presenter of the show, and Butt broke the news to Fred that his father had died. He added a suggestion that he close the show for a while but the decision was made to continue. It isn't easy being nutty on stage when your off-stage thoughts are anything but . . .

Fred and Adele had a tremendous last night in *Stop Flirting*, and from all over the auditorium there were cries of 'Come back soon!', 'Give my regards to Broadway!' . . . 'Don't forget to write!'. They sailed away for their first glimpse of America in twenty months. George Gershwin, they learned on arrival, had finally scored the musical comedy he had promised them, *Lady Be Good*. His brother Ira had supplied the lyrics. Vinton Freedly, an actor with whom Fred had shared a dressing room, had gone into partnership with Alex Aarons and they presented the show at the Liberty Theatre, New York in December 1924.

It was in *Lady Be Good* that the Astaires made their triumphant return to London. Sir Alfred Butt had refurbished the famous Empire Theatre in Leicester Square in anticipation. The show would, as matters turned out, be its last. They opened in April 1926 and took the town once again, Fred contributing a solo for the first time and confessing that he kicked himself for not including one before. The proposed sale and demolition of the Empire was announced to a surprised public after six months, and immediately there was a run on tickets for the last night, still three months away. When the day dawned at last, January 22nd 1927, Fred received a telephone call. 'Mr Astaire?' 'Yes.' 'Just a moment, sir, the Prince of Wales would like to speak to you . . .' Convinced this was a joke, Fred was on the point of saying 'Tell him I'm not in,' when a familiar voice said 'Hullo, Astaire . . .' The rest of the conversation raised Fred's hair, which was already showing signs that it would not be, forever, in plentiful supply. The Prince wanted a box for the last performance, a demand such as he was rather inclined to make. It throws the theatre into panic, since it means they have to telephone a theatre-goer who has taken the trouble to book ahead and ask him to give up his seats. When you tell him why, he'll be less inclined to oblige than

to want to come and join in the fun. A decade later when Edward
was King he wanted seats for a Noël Coward sell-out. With
considerable difficulty the Master complied. He was, understandably, not too happy when the King came backstage after the
play and spent half an hour in Gertrude Lawrence's dressing
room, having bypassed the author and co-star. Coward telephoned the Palace to remonstrate, however gently, and one of
those 'spokesmen' offered the defence: 'After all, he is King.' 'In
my theatre,' snapped Noël, '*I* am King!' On this *Lady Be Good*
occasion, Solly Joel gave up his box and a royal time was had by
all. It was a superlative last night, the evening ending in St
James's Palace where the Astaires were the guests of the Prince
until four a.m.

Fred and Adele had bought a British motor car. They took it
back with them to New York and were the owners of the only
white Rolls Royce on Broadway. Rolls and Royce might have
engineered their career, so smoothly did it run. In New York,
Alex Aarons and Vinton Freedly had built a new theatre and,
joining the first syllables of their first names, had called it the
'Alvin'. They presented the Astaires in *Funny Face*, again with
music and lyrics by the Gershwins. It opened at the Alvin on
November 22nd 1927. What the *Funny Face* company went
through backstage before the opening night is Magic Circle stuff,
not for the uninitiated. At one point in the rehearsals Fred had
remarked: 'This damn turkey hasn't got a prayer, I'm going into
the horse business!' About his work he was, perhaps, over
serious—Adele called him 'Moaning Minnie'. The turkey was a
smash hit.

The more dedicated Moaning Minnie Fred became to perfec-
tion in performance, the more un-dedicated became Adele. On
the second night of the new success she turned up both late and
lit, having downed more than one social cocktail. This is the sin
we artists never commit, or if we do we don't commit it again.
We don't get the chance—just the sack. Up to now Adele had
never partaken unduly, not so that Minnie would notice. To be
sure she didn't do it again, and in the hope she'd get by without

incident tonight, Fred gave her a push—to say nothing of a shove, a niff of smelling salts that would fell an ox ... and another shove on to the stage. 'I sang most of the song', he records, 'pulling her round on a toy wagon, so there was no serious trouble up to that point. But when we started to dance ... oh, brother! Or sister!' When they came off stage he had to slap her face before she'd go on to take a bow. When they came off again she said 'You hit me!' 'Yes,' said Fred, and bundled her into her dressing room to change. When she met him at their next entrance she said again, 'You hit me!' 'I had to,' said Fred, by now beset with remorse, 'Forget it, I'll give you twenty bucks tomorrow.' They got through the evening, though not, it must be admitted, having given of their best. Fred apologized to his sister next day for having had to be cruel with kindness in mind. Said Adele 'Where's my twenty bucks?' She got them.

Funny Face opened in London at the Prince's Theatre (subsequently called the Shaftesbury) in November of 1928. Again it was a smash hit, the words on this occasion having a side connotation. A gas main blew and the streets around the theatre became a mashed up no-man's-land. The show closed for a few days but, for some time after the reopening, the ladies in their evening dresses and the men in their tails were clambering over boards on their way to the Prince's to see the Astaires. It's as well they were popular.

Adele Astaire had been pursued by the males for some time—there would have had to be something wrong with the males if she hadn't been. On the last night of *Funny Face* she met Lord Charles Cavendish, the second son of the Duke of Devonshire. He followed them home to America.

The Astaires played in a show called *Smiles* for Ziegfeld—and everyone frowned on it. Two prophetic things happened though, during the short run. Alex Aarons asked Fred to choreograph a number for *Girl Crazy*. 'Embraceable you' was the song, the couple singing and dancing would be Alan Kearns and an up-and-coming juvenile named Ginger Rogers. Ginger and Fred went out together several times; they even danced to Eddie

Duchin's band. The second prophetic happening was that Fred choreographed, for himself in his own show, a number in which he aimed a stick at and shot down with taps a line of chorus men. Later, this four a.m. idea of Fred's inspired Irving Berlin to write the title song of the movie *Top Hat*.

Smiles, the flop, was followed by *The Band Wagon*, a palpable hit. Adele wanted to retire at a peak, and this was the peak. She married Charles Cavendish and went to live in a castle in Ireland. Fred, like many another male in life's song and dance, found himself in the position of having to make other arrangements. He never would have a partner to equal Adele. 'A thousand laughs I've found from having you around ...' he had sung to her in *Funny Face*. The song had ended with the words 'Though you're no Follies beauty, you're great for kitchen duty ...' It was unlikely that Lady Cavendish would have an opportunity to prove it in that Irish castle, but Fred had to accept that, for the theatre, her enthusiasm had burnt itself out. The genius that had begun to glow in Fred would refuel itself, as is the way of genius. He was sad to lose Adele, but genius has a way, too, of not suffering a lack of interest with too much patience. 'I was very glad that she retired,' he said. 'She didn't like to practise very much and I was glad to see her do what she wanted to do ... She wanted to retire ... she did. She did and she never had any urge to come back.'

Adele wasn't the only one with matrimony in mind. Fred was in hot, if prolonged, pursuit of a charmer named Phyllis Potter. She continued to hold off. Fred made his solo debut in *The Gay Divorce*—with words and music by Cole Porter. Adele sent him a telegram that read 'NOW MINNIE DON'T FORGET TO MOAN'. Fred then signed a movie contract with RKO, which clinched it with his lady. 'You'll have all those girls after you,' said Phyllis.'I won't be after them,' he reassured her. 'Yes,' she said, 'but I might spend a lot of time wondering if you are.'

They got married and hied them to the celluloid city. RKO lent Fred to MGM first, for a movie called *Dancing Lady* starring Joan Crawford and Clark Gable. Fred made a very brief appearance in it, playing himself. He thought it might break him in for his first with RKO, *Flying Down to Rio*. Before the opening of this one he travelled to England to repeat his stage perform-ance in *The Gay Divorce*. The press were kinder to him than they had been in New York. He recalled the notices there: 'Some of the critics took great glee in saying "This show proves that two Astaires are better than one ..." and "Fred seemed to be looking off into the wings for his sister to come and rescue him ..." I had to go through all that stuff ...' I saw *The Gay Divorce* in Birmingham on its way to London and I didn't notice Fred doing any glancing into the wings. I thought he seemed very happy being an enormous hit on his own.

Fred didn't think much of his chances in films, nor did the moguls who were making them, until the public reacted to *Flying Down to Rio*. When he took Ginger Rogers on to the dance floor for the first time—the screen dance floor—to do the carioca he played a cinematic trump card. Did he, in fact, need a partner? I can only say that, as far as I am concerned, whenever I saw Fred and Ginger dancing on the screen I never looked at Ginger—that is, apart from the odd, fleeting glance when she raised a long, loose skirt to show silk. Maybe it was her outer garments that put me off. It certainly put Fred off on more than one occasion. There was the famous episode of the feathered dress Ginger chose in the 'Cheek to cheek' number in *Top Hat*. 'I never,' said Fred, 'saw so many feathers in my life. It was like a snow storm. They were floating around like millions of moths ... I had feathers in my eyes, my ears, my mouth ... all over the front of my suit which happened to be black tails ...' Off set, he and Hermes Pan, the choreographer, rewrote the lyrics Irving Berlin had written to the song and sang quietly to themselves:

> FEATHERS, I HATE FEATHERS ...
> AND I HATE THEM SO THAT I CAN HARDLY SPEAK ...
> AND I'LL NEVER FIND THE HAPPINESS I SEEK ...
> WITH THOSE CHICKEN FEATHERS,
> DANCING CHEEK TO CHEEK!

Fred with Ginger Rogers in the memorable 'feathers' sequence in *Top Hat*.

Astaire was a keen golfer, as the superb sequence in *Carefree*
shows, and he had a genuis for keeping an eye on the studio ball.
His acting became polished, the comedy glinted brightly; his
singing was pleasant enough and gave, moreover, the fullest
meaning to the lyrics, song writers loving him for it. He even
became a song writer, or half a one, a composer. A man named
Shelley wrote some words and the Benny Goodman band plus the
Sextet accompanied Fred when he recorded 'Just like taking
candy from a baby'. For one song Johnny Mercer supplied the
lyrics:

> I'M BUILDING UP TO AN AWFUL LET DOWN
> BY PLAYING AROUND WITH YOU;
> YOU'RE BREAKING DOWN MY TERRIFIC BUILD UP
> BY TREATING ME AS YOU DO . . .

Astaire was not the only singer to record this, it became a minor
hit.

He was an accomplished pianist. In *Follow The Fleet*, to show
the audience that he is, in fact, playing, he had the front of the
upright piano removed with the excuse that he is tuning it. He
plays and you see the hammers—no trickery here.

It was a long and interesting progress. A four-year-old who
didn't much want to dance, growing up to be a man who did, and
decided that slackness, if you did dance, wouldn't do. Hard
worker into Moaning Minnie perfectionist . . . Perfectionizing
leaves you lonely, which is why not many persist in it. Fred
Astaire did, and became a beautifully skilled artist: actor (his
comedy was very nice indeed); singer with a knack of meaning
what he sang (and the songs were by Irving Berlin, Kern and
Fields, the Gershwins—the very best); pianist with fingers almost
as deft as his dancing feet; composer of some twenty recorded
numbers; innovative choreographer; dancer supreme who
danced as he acted, right in character—from the phoney Russian
Petrov with his balletic comments in *Shall We Dance?* to the
brash, failed-hoofer-turned-sailor in *Follow The Fleet*.

Each of the dances he introduced in films had its own individual appeal, its original steps ... the Piccolino, the Continental, the Shorty George, the Yam—all delightfully different. 'Choreography by Hermes Pan', it said, but I can't but feel that Minnie had a hand, or two feet. It is likely that, between them, a great deal of midnight oil—or studio lampage—was consumed. Thomas Carlyle would have smiled knowingly, we feel. He might even have danced a buck and wing.

I was sorry never to have seen Astaire on a stage again. But stage performances pass in a night, while celluloid (now that nitrate is out) is forever. I feel the same about Astaire as I feel about Robert Donat. Beautiful he was on a stage, but if he hadn't gone into pictures we would have nothing of him left. Nothing of Fred Astaire? Imagine! As it is we have a wonderful treasure house—*Roberta, Top Hat, Follow the Fleet, Swing Time, Shall We Dance?, A Damsel in Distress* ... This last film I saw at a late night movie house in New York, going in a Moaning Minnie, for some reason I can't recall, and coming out walking on air a foot above Broadway. And Ginger wasn't even in it. She was back with him in *Carefree* and in *The Story of Vernon and Irene Castle*. He had a stream of partners from then on. In *Broadway Melody of 1940* he danced 'Begin the Beguine' with Eleanor Powell; he made two films with Bing, *Holiday Inn* and *Blue Skies*. Then came *Easter Parade*. Fred had more or less retired from dancing, but Gene Kelly broke an ankle playing with some kids and Fred stepped in.

The Berkeleys of Broadway brought him together with Ginger again and for the last time. Here, it was she who stepped in for a very sick Judy Garland. In *Royal Wedding* he danced up the wall, across the ceiling and down the other side, this time with the help of trickery. *The Band Wagon* was the souped up screen version, unrecognizable except for one or two of the songs, of his last stage show with Adele.

Phyllis Astaire and Fred were a very private husband and wife. She died in 1954. They had two children, Ava and Fred Jr. Fred remained alone for more than twenty-five years, and then in

1980, at the age of eighty-one, this perennially young character, appropriately, married youth. The second Mrs Astaire was a thirty-seven-year-old jockey whose name had been Robyn Smith. Fred had continued to act, playing straight parts in movies, enjoying himself. Good as he was in these parts, many an actor can do them. I don't know of one who could begin to match the magic of Astaire when he takes off. How he carries us along . . . up, up . . . and round . . . heady stuff, you have the feeling you have tasted champagne, you put out your glass for more . . .

Fred Astaire set little or no store by the past. Those of us who do thank him for the magic and for putting a degree of it on celluloid so that it will always be there. What we have in those cans is unrepeatable. Reason enough, I think, to call it genius.

Before the opening of *Stop Flirting* – in May, 1923 – Fred and Adele Astaire danced for the press on the roof of the Savoy Hotel.

LORENZ HART
Little Man Blue

Larry Hart listening to a setting for some of his words by his lifetime
collaborator, Dick Rodgers.

LORENZ HART

REMEMBER THE YOUTH 'MID SNOW AND ICE
WHO BORE THE BANNER WITH THE STRANGE DEVICE
'EXCELSIOR!'
WHOSE MOTTO APPLIES TO THOSE WHO DWELL
IN RICHMOND HILL OR NEW ROCHELLE,
IN CHELSEA OR
IN SUTTON PLACE!
YOU'VE GOT TO REACH THE HEIGHTS TO WIN THE RACE . . .

Lorenz Hart who wrote those words was barely five feet tall, even wearing elevated shoes. But reach the lyrical heights, he did—and scaled them, rhyme after rhyme. 'On your toes', of which the words speak the verse, is one of something approaching five hundred songs by Rodgers and Hart. According to the man who wrote the music, Richard Rodgers, the lyrics of Lorenz Hart 'helped to change the face of musical theatre'. As the *New York Times* expressed it: 'Not lesser of the two was Larry Hart whose facility with simple words added something felicitous to our lives.'

Lorenz Milton Hart—the second name not, I think, given with any poetic intent—was born in New York on May 2nd, 1895. Two years later his brother Teddy arrived to complete the family. Teddy always wished he could write, Lorenz—or Larry—longed to be a comedian. Teddy became the comedian and Larry, to quote the *New York Times* again, 'the laureate of lyrics'.

The Hart parents were German-Jewish. His mother Freda, all four feet ten of her, had been stage struck but had made a recovery. Father, Max, was loud-mouthed and foul-mouthed and altogether hail-fellow-ill-met. Yet the sum total seems to have been a strange, bluff charm that enabled him to make many a fast buck with questions neither asked nor answered. The Hart children, not exactly born with silver spoons in their mouths, had them thrust down their gullets at an early age. Max Hart made money and spent it—lent it too, if you wanted it. Such open-handedness will make Dracula socially acceptable. Moreover, the Hart house was open house, with anyone and everyone welcome at all hours. Young Larry was brought up in a domestic—to use a word he would coin later—'hobo-hemia' in which discipline was a non-word. He was even encouraged to drink.

Summer camp played a great part in the lives of young New Yorkers and Larry was in demand as a laughter maker. When boys are out for laughter they don't mind the appearance of the lad who provokes it. From this raggety, half-pint-sized gnome with the huge head and pointed ears came such a glow of personal charm that he became a leader. Raggety he was because he had only the clothes he arrived in; his trunk—it took two to carry it—was packed to the lid with books, which caused him to be nicknamed 'Shakespeare Hart'. Like the Bard's Autolycus, Larry, at camp, was a snapper-up of unconsidered trifles such as socks, a carelessness which led to his other nickname, 'Dirty neck'. He couldn't, it seems, both wash and read. Soap and water do call for discipline in the beginning, while reading asks only a hungry mind. Larry Hart stuffed his as other kids pile in the pie *à la mode*.

It has been said the Harts were descended from the German poet Heinrich Heine. Be that as it may or may not—and Larry had no time for such claims—his knowledge of the tongue led to his translating German plays and operettas into English for the Shubert Brothers. He began to have some of his own way with the lyrics, not merely translating but adapting them, cutting them new clothes to fit. The Shuberts paid him next to nothing, which didn't matter, but they also failed to appreciate the artistry in what he was doing, which did. Larry became restless for recognition, for theatrical adventure, new lyrical paths.

At this point, when Larry was in his twenty-fourth year, a friend, Philip Leavitt, brought to the house a sixteen-year-old composer named Richard Rodgers. He and Hart lived round the corner from one another, had done for years without meeting. Larry Hart came to the door. He was wearing evening trousers, carpet slippers, any old shirt and more than a day's growth of beard. Leavitt left the two together, Rodgers playing his compositions, Hart impressed with the newness of harmonic approach. According to Leavitt, 'it was love at first sight'.

Referring again to Carlyle's contention that 'genius is a transcendent capacity of taking trouble', if genius ends there Larry Hart simply doesn't qualify. His talent was like forked-lightning and the following thunder. By the time the rumble had died away his work was done—it was almost that electric. Revision was a bore to him, he hated retouching. If you needed three extra choruses he would, if you could find him, produce them in as few minutes even with other music playing. His facility was staggering. As for taking trouble, the greatest trouble Shakespeare Hart ever took was to 'put an enemy in his mouth to steal away his brains'. Rodgers and Hart began an enthusiastic partnership. 'Enthusiastic', at least, would have been the word for Larry; earnestness was Dick's forte.

Richard Rodgers was the most unlikely man to make music. He had a disciplined, nine-till-five mind and the financial feel of a Rockefeller, which was just as well for Larry. Without Rodgers' application and acumen we would have been minus two thirds of Hart's lyrical output. Equally, without Hart's lyrics there was a serious possibility that Rodgers might have ended up in babies' underwear! Even with Hart's lyrics it was touch and go, but more of this in a moment. The catalytic Philip Leavitt gave them one more shove on fate's behalf. He introduced them to Lew Fields, late of the Vaudeville team Weber and Fields. Lew Fields was presenting shows on Broadway and actually bought one of their songs. They couldn't believe their luck when, in August 1919, he put it into his new show. The music wasn't memorable but the lyric was a foretaste of the verbal potions the puckish Hart would administer . . .

I'LL GO TO HELL FOR YA
OR PHILADELPHIA—
ANY OLD PLACE WITH YOU . . . !

'Any old place with you' was the first published Rodgers and Hart song. They thought they were away. In the theatre you are never away until the day you snuff it, but this was a lesson yet to be learnt. After this first heady bump against success they spent five years in the wilderness. There was wide open opportunity for writers to work for nothing. University shows—they were both at Columbia—camp shows . . . that's if you didn't expect to make an honest buck. Luckily, Rodgers, too, was comfortably placed in a middle-class family setting. His father and brother were doctors. His preference for music was indulged but the honest buck would mean professional acceptance, and like Larry Hart he craved recognition. Also, he was now twenty-three and Larry was thirty. Suddenly babies' underwear loomed large in that he was offered a woolly job and was about to take it up. Then came one more opportunity. To work for nothing. The prestigious Theatre Guild who had built a new theatre and needed curtains thought they would earn a dishonest buck by getting actors to put on a show for the love of it and hand over the proceeds to them. It was the name 'Theatre Guild' that swung it, as the Theatre Guild knew it would, and instead of 'babies' underwear by Rodgers' it became, yet again, 'music and lyrics by Rodgers and Hart'. *The Garrick Gaieties* they called the show, which was to have only two performances, a Sunday afternoon and evening.

The workers for nothing scored a signal success and wondered how to cash in a fortune in applause. During the week the Garrick Theatre was presenting the Lunts, Alfred Lunt and Lynn Fontanne, in their highly successful comedy *The Guardsman*. Only youth would have had the temerity to suggest Mr and Mrs Lunt move out. Youth did, and the Lunts gave place—graciously or not, we can't be sure—to *The Garrick Gaieties*. The hit of the show was a song the world's top publisher Max Dreyfus had turned down—'Manhattan'. Larry Hart had gone to town, so to speak, on the

lyrics. The sense continuation after the rhyme was becoming a trade
mark . . .

> SUMMER JOURNEYS TO NIAG'RA
> AND TO OTHER PLACES AGGRA-
> VATE ALL OUR CARES . . .

I have mentioned Larry's hatred of tampering with a lyric after
the first scribble down. As Dick Rodgers' wife expressed it,
Larry's first thought was usually better than another person's
fiftieth. In 'Manhattan' occur the lines:

> WE'LL BATHE AT BRIGHTON,
> THE FISH YOU'LL FRIGHTEN
> WHEN YOU'RE IN!
> YOUR BATHING SUIT SO THIN
> WILL MAKE THE SHELLFISH GRIN,
> FIN TO FIN . . .

One can imagine the strict Rodgers mentioning that shellfish have
no fins but by that time Larry would have been out of the house and
in the furthest bar. A line that had a deep meaning for me was the one
about 'We'll starve together, dear, in Childs' . . . Childs' was a chain
of restaurants where you could eat reasonably if you had to—I used
to eat hash there before going to Henry Miller's Theatre to play in
French Without Tears. I went into Childs' nearly broke and came out
starving every night. In *The Garrick Gaieties*, 'Manhattan' was sung
by Sterling Holloway, whom Walt Disney was later to cast as the
stork who brought Dumbo.

The Garrick Gaieties ran for more than two hundred performances. Herb Fields, son of Lew, had become a third in the
partnership, and from an idea given to him by Larry Hart he wrote
Dearest Enemy, a book show about the Civil War. They had finished
this long ago and hawked it about without success. 'Score by
Rodgers and Hart' had meant nothing. 'Score by Rodgers and Hart
of *The Garrick Gaieties*' was a different kettle of theatrical fish, with

or without the fins. *Dearest Enemy* ran for nearly three hundred performances. While it was still running, into Broadway came one more show with book by Herb Fields, music and lyrics by Rodgers and Hart, *The Girl Friend*. The title song was the breath of the twenties and is still much played and imitated when a Charleston tempo is called for. The score also contained the perennial-to-be, 'Blue room'.

All successful revues were inclined to go to a second edition. The new *Garrick Gaieties* opened two months before *The Girl Friend*. The hit song, again sung by Sterling Holloway in duet with a lady, was 'Mountain Greenery'. The rhymes leap and play like firelight...

> HERE A GIRL CAN MAP HER OWN
> LIFE WITHOUT A CHAPERONE,
> IT'S SO GOOD IT MUST BE IMMORAL...

Quite daring for 1926! The lad will take his ukulele...

> YOU CAN BET YOUR LIFE ITS TONE
> BEATS A JASCHA HEIFETZ TONE...

Rodgers and Hart were now invited to London to write words and music for *Lido Lady*. They travelled via Venice to pick up some local colour but they didn't get on with their boss, Jack Hulbert, and wrote a poor score for him. Which was the cause and which the effect is not certain. They wrote the score for *Peggy Ann* which opened in New York on December 27th 1926 and ran for 333 performances. The next night opened the Ziegfeld show *Betsy* with their score which ran for thirty-nine performances. Such are the ups and downs of the roller coaster called theatre. The ups had outnumbered the downs. In little more than eighteen months Rodgers and Hart had scored, in both senses, five hits on Broadway.

The flop in London rankled and when Charles B. Cochran sent for them to return there they packed a trunkful of determined intentions and travelled, once more, via the continent. One day in

Paris they found themselves in a taxi with two ladies. As Paris taxis will, it missed a collision by centimetres. Dick Rodgers remembers that one lady gasped, 'My heart stood still!' 'What a great title!' said Larry, making a note on the back of something. They made a great song of it and popped it into Cochran's *'One Dam Thing After Another* ('damn' spelt without the final 'n' as a sop to the prudish. In fact, the show became known as O.D.T.A.A.!). Jessie Matthews sang 'My heart stood still' and Edythe Baker played it on her white piano.

For some time Herb Fields, Richard Rodgers and Larry Hart had played with the idea of translating a Mark Twain novel into a musical. *A Connecticut Yankee in King Arthur's Court*, Twain had called it, but he didn't have to worry about people ringing up the box office to get tickets. The modern adaptors shortened it to *A Connecticut Yankee*. It followed *Peggy Ann* into the Vanderbilt Theatre in November 1927. It isn't only the money men who tend not to know what's what in the creative sphere. Lew Fields, who directed *A Connecticut Yankee*, fought hard to have one of the songs cut. The writers fought harder and 'Thou swell' stayed in to become the hit of the show.

Present Arms followed and scored 155 performances. It contained the Rodgers and Hart standard-to-be 'You took advantage of me'. (For the first night treatment of this see the piece on Busby Berkeley.) *Spring Is Here* had a modest run. The title would later inspire one of Hart's most piognant lyrics but not for this show. It did contain a very successful number called 'With a song in my heart'—a good, commercial melody and a lyric which Larry hated.

Their last effort for Ziegfeld had ended in near disaster, but 1929 being the year it was the money folk were more often jumping out of windows than investing in shows. Ziggy's invitation to write the score for *Simple Simon* was eagerly accepted. A further cogent reason for Dick Rodgers was that he was about to marry Dorothy Feiner whom he had met on his first trip back from Europe.

Cockie—Charles B. Cochran—had refurbished the Adelphi Theatre in London and now invited Rodgers and Hart to travel over and create the score for *Evergreen*. Rodgers thought they should share a house, Larry being as elusive as he was, and Dorothy agreed. She discovered at once that Larry was no ordinary house guest. The accommodation they rented in Regent's Park was sumptuous enough but there was a hot water problem. There was plenty if you didn't waste it. She was careful to warn Larry about this and he promised to take note. On arrival at the house he turned on the taps for a bath and promptly forgot. Dorothy received a call from a neighbour who informed her that hot water was gushing from the overflow pipe down into York Terrace. Larry was deeply apologetic. The next day the episode was repeated. *Evergreen* opened in December 1930 and ran for 250 performances. The hit of the show was a song Ziegfeld had thrown out of his revue, 'Dancing on the ceiling', which Jessie Matthews sang in a superb upside-down setting.

It is not, of course, only men with nine-till-five minds that marry. It rarely happens that they don't, however, and when they do they seem to be able to order matrimony as they order everything else. What do you do when you have an all-round-the-clock mind? Larry Hart never did achieve the settled domestic happiness that came to Dick Rodgers as of right. His father had died and he lived with his mother for his entire home life. He proposed marriage more than once to more than one lady. Their rejection of him was not, I think, on account of his looks. Nanette Guilford, the Metropolitan Opera soprano to whom he proposed quite soon after Rodgers married, attended a Hollywood party and recalled that, amid the handsomest stars in the colony, he held the floor with sheer personality. A lady reporter who interviewed him was unable to remember his height afterwards. 'He's very small isn't he?' asked a colleague. 'Small? I don't think so, no. He's . . . quite tall . . .' Later when the reporter saw him again she was amazed to notice his shortness. Dorothy Rodgers said of him 'He was so generous, so warm-hearted, so full of enthusiasm that everybody loved him.' But not, it seems, enough. Nanette Guilford had divorced one genius, she said, and had decided to stay single. Frances Manson, a story editor at Columbia, gave as her reason for not accepting Larry that she didn't want to wind up drinking as much as he did. Unacceptable matrimonially because he drank . . . did he drink because of the unacceptability?

When you are alone, rich and a touch alcoholic you never lack for hangers-on. One of these was a certain Milton Bender. The first name he shared with Larry, something that occurs to me only now. It was never used with either of them, Bender always being known as 'Doc'. He had been, of all things, a dentist. He was popular with no one except Larry Hart whom he had cultivated since summer camp days. Practising dentists are sometimes not popular but this one seems to have practised everything but dentistry. He has been named, in print, as a procurer. Whether Hart's sexual proclivities underwent a change or whether it was merely that Doc Bender was trying to drum up business will never, I think, be certain. There was no doubt whatever that the association with this character was lamented by all Larry's real friends. He was a satanic presence —and he seemed always to be there . . .

It was natural that Rodgers and Hart should be in demand by Hollywood. Their first visit there was abortive. Their second produced the only movie they handled to their satisfaction, '*Love Me Tonight*' starring Maurice Chevalier. 'Mimi . . . you funny little good-for-nothing Mimi . . .' they contributed to the great man's permanent repertoire.

Dick Rodgers found that pinning Larry down to work was like trying to jam your thumb on a blob of mercury. In Hollywood as in London, the only hope seemed to be to keep him under the same roof. Dorothy, again, found this trying in the extreme. 'Larry decided that his contribution would be the liquor,' she said. 'He would buy it and he would dispense it.' Dinner parties were a problem. Larry would be in the kitchen dispensing cocktails. 'One for him, one for the cook . . .' said Dorothy '. . . and pretty soon, there would be no dinner.' She added with restraint: 'It was difficult to keep house for man like that.' Larry smoked cigars, which were often a foot long. He would stand at the window dreaming about something . . . it might be Mimi . . . and burning a hole in the curtains without knowing it.

Hollywood was not, on the whole, a happy time for any of them. Rodgers and Hart wrote the score for *The Phantom President* and got

on not at all well with George M. Cohan. Cohan was too much of a
legend. He had been a highly successful Broadway producer of his
own shows, a tremendous star actor and composer. How do you
write songs for the man who wrote 'Over there' and 'I'm a yankee
doodle dandy'? The answer was they couldn't, and didn't to any
purpose. The film was not a success. In *Hallelujah, I'm a Bum* Hart
wrote a beautiful lyric which he might have been addressing to
Frances Manson who was in the process of turning him down. I
wonder if Dick Rodgers knew, and not only in this instance, what
inner thinking he was setting to music...

YOU ARE TOO BEAUTIFUL, MY DEAR, TO BE TRUE
AND I AM TOO DRUNK WITH BEAUTY:
DRUNK WITH ILLUSION THAT THE ONE WHO CARESSED YOU
REALLY POSSESSED YOU TOO:
YOU ARE TOO BEAUTIFUL FOR ONE MAN ALONE,
FOR ONE LUCKY FOOL TO BE WITH
WHEN THERE ARE OTHER MEN
WITH EYES OF THEIR OWN TO SEE WITH:
LOVES DOES NOT STAND SHARING,
NOT IF ONE CARES . . .

The insecurity of the lover who sings:

HAVE YOU BEEN COMPARING
MY EVERY KISS WITH THEIRS?

The recovery of nonchalance:

IF, ON THE OTHER HAND, I'M FAITHFUL TO YOU
IT'S NOT THROUGH A SENSE OF DUTY:
YOU ARE TOO BEAUTIFUL
AND I AM TOO DRUNK WITH BEAUTY!

Back on Broadway, Billy Rose was spending a fortune of money
men's money in gutting the interior of the Hippodrome on 44th
Street and Sixth Avenue. He put in a three-ring circus and engaged
the Paul Whiteman Orchestra and Jimmy Durante—the show was

called, not inappropriately, *Jumbo*. It didn't run. Circus shows are not supposed to by theatrical superstition, if you believe in it. But Rodgers and Hart contributed three great songs, 'My romance', 'Little girl blue' and the one that contained Larry's sophisticated but ecstatic tribute to 'The Most Beautiful Girl in the World'.

On Your Toes was a flop in London. To Rodgers and Hart this was one more down on the roller-coaster, in New York they had run for a respectable three-hundred-and-something performances. It was the best musical I had ever seen. Today, it has been equalled for me, never bettered. For the first time a musical contained a ballet. It was Larry Hart's idea that Rodgers should write *Slaughter on Tenth Avenue*. Maybe he figured out that with Dick hard at work and not needing a lyric he, Larry, would be able to put in drinking time. Composer and lyric writer also shared the book with George Abbott. I think Larry may have seen himself as the plain little Mr Cohn who writes the jazz ballet. At first the head of the classical music school rejects such an idea. The pupils have just sung a peach of a song praising Bach, Beethoven and Brahms. The little fellow picks up his music and makes a deeply hurt exit with the words: 'Never mind! Some day the name of Cohn will be familiar too!' *On Your Toes* had some beautiful lyrics: the sentimental 'There's a small hotel', filed away after being cut from *Jumbo*, was neatly leavened with Hartian wit and humour . . .

PRETTY WINDOW CURTAINS MADE OF CHINTZ
IN OUR MAKE BELIEVE LAND;
ON THE WALL ARE SEVERAL CHEERFUL PRINTS
OF GRANT AND GROVER CLEVELAND;
GO DOWN INTO THE PARLOUR AND FEAST YOUR EYES
ON THE MOOSE HEAD ON THE WALL!
PERHAPS YOU'D LIKE TO PLAY THE ORGAN?
THEY TUNE IT EV'RY OTHER FALL!
THE GARDEN WILL BE LIKE ADAM AND EVE-LAND;
NO, THEY NEVER DID GO IN FOR CARRIAGE TRADE,
THEY GET WHAT IS KNOWN AS 'MARRIAGE TRADE' . . .

I sailed for New York in September 1937. At the earliest possible moment I made bee-lines for every Broadway theatre with matinées that didn't coincide with ours. One such possibility was *Babes in Arms*, a Rodgers and Hart musical par excellence. The score was not to be believed: in one ineffable afternoon I heard for the first time 'Where or when', 'Johnny one note', 'My funny valentine', 'All at once', 'Babes in arms', 'I wish I were in love again' and 'The lady is a tramp'! Speaking of this lady, Larry Hart is surely the only daredevil who could have rhymed 'bad' with 'Noël Ca'ad' and got away with it.

Another lyrical *tour de force* was the song sung by Rolly Pickert and Grace MacDonald. Grace MacDonald I adored, falling completely in love with her, I followed her all over New York. Finally I caught up with her and found her to be rather snooty and not at all the girl I had dreamt up. That's youth and that's love. This is lyric writing:

THE SLEEPLESS NIGHTS,
THE DAILY FIGHTS,
THE QUICK TOBOGGAN WHEN YOU REACH THE HEIGHTS;
I MISS THE KISSES AND I MISS THE BITES,
I WISH I WERE IN LOVE AGAIN!
THE BROKEN DATES,
THE ENDLESS WAITS,
THE LOVELY LOVING AND THE HATEFUL HATES,
THE CONVERSATION WITH THE FLYING PLATES—
I WISH I WERE IN LOVE AGAIN!

In the second chorus occur the classic lines:

WHEN LOVE CONGEALS,
IT SOON REVEALS
THE FAINT AROMA OF PERFORMING SEALS . . .

While *Babes in Arms* was still packing the Shubert Theatre I used to see Dick Rodgers and Larry Hart bobbing in and out of Sardi's. Rodgers was thirty-five, Hart was forty-two—both old gentlemen to me. George S. Kaufman was there too, and Moss Hart. All were involved in the new production at the Alvin Theatre. President Roosevelt was to be shown on the stage, portrayed by George M. Cohan. The name of the show, already up in lights, was *I'd Rather Be Right*. I didn't realize then, as a skinny lad who didn't know whether he could afford to go to Sardi's or couldn't afford not to, that backstage at the Alvin all Hell was breaking loose. Cohan didn't like the songs, perhaps because he thought he should have been asked to write them. He did have grounds for some complaint: he didn't even get to sing the hit song 'Have you met Miss Jones?', which went to the juvenile. The legendary Mr Cohan pulled his weight at the box office, though. I had to buy my ticket from a tout, it cost me six dollars—twenty-two and sixpence.

I hated leaving New York in the spring of 1938 with all this Rodgers and Hartistry going on. The happy cast of kids—Alfred Drake was the old man at twenty-four—in *Babes in Arms* at the Shubert gave place to the heavenly Zorina. *I Married an Angel* was the name of the show. I had seen Vera Zorina in London in *On Your Toes*, and not to be able to see her again in *I Married an Angel* was cruelty to the very young and in love. I had fallen out of love with Grace MacDonald from *Babes in Arms* but in any case I had an infinite capacity.

Larry's brother Teddy Hart was a success on Broadway. He had made a hit in *Three Men on a Horse*. I saw him in *Room Service* which was well into its running stride in New York during 1937. It was the likeness between his brother and the comedian Jimmy Savo that gave Larry the idea for the musical *The Boys from Syracuse*, a free adaptation of Shakespeare's *A Comedy of Errors*. *The Boys from Syracuse* opened in November 1938 at the Alvin Theatre and was to run for 236 performances. If it hadn't been for a drama of errors being enacted in Europe it might have run and run like the Dromios.

Too Many Girls opened in October 1939. It contained a touch

A month before the November 1938 opening of *The Boys from Syracuse* the *Herald Tribune* printed this caricature of Larry with Dick Rodgers and George Abbott, the director, in conference at the Algonquin Hotel in New York.

of Larry at his best:

> I LIKE TO RECOGNISE THE TUNE,
> I LIKE TO SAVVY WHAT THE BAND IS PLAYING,
> I KEEP SAYING
> MUST YOU BURY THE TUNE?

The lyric includes the astonishing couplet:

> WHEN SHE HEARS THOSE CHORDS OF EDDIE DUCHINS,
> ELSA MAXWELL QUIVERS WITH HER TWO CHINS!

Around this time, the turning of the thirties into the forties, there appeared these words written by Dorothy Kilgallen, in the New York *Journal American*:

> Larry Hart is a quick, dark, darting little man with pointed ears, a gleeful laugh and the face of a smart faun sitting in on a poker game with the angels. It is no secret that he composes lyrics, for he and Dick Rodgers usually have a hit musical or two kicking around the Broadway boards, but it is a great mystery when he composes his rhymes, for no one has ever caught him working, not even his mother with whom he lives. He is one of the more ubiquitous of the café crowd, noticeable at the ballet, the first nights, the opera, the more gilded soirées and at midnight in Sardi's. He loves the music of opera but thinks that, as an art form, it is ridiculous and he and Paul Muni once agreed at a Metropolitan matinée that Tristan and Isolde should be performed only for the blind. Larry never shaves himself and never writes letters. He adores and bosses his brother Teddy, the comedian, hates Hollywood and is enchanted with Vivienne Segal because she has a vocabulary as colourful as his own. The other evening he invited Betty Grable and Desi Arnaz to his house for dinner, then forgot to show up himself. No one was even slightly surprised at his absence—especially Larry . . .

It is a fairly complete picture. Vivienne Segal starred in the 1940 joint effort *Pal Joey*. John O'Hara had suggested he adapt some of his stories. Rodgers was having increasing difficulty finding Larry Hart, and now he was going to have track down an equally elusive John O'Hara.

Pal Joey as a subject followed the pattern for Rodgers and Hart of striving always for something that hadn't been attempted before. The story had a middle-aged lady keeping the young hero who hadn't a saving grace except one that, theatrically, used to be unmentionable. How would the audience take it? How would the critics take it, who had the power not to let the audience get a look in? Who would play the anti-hero? The word hadn't been invented, there were no characters to apply it to. Now, one was here and waiting. There was a young lad about Broadway named Gene Kelly. He was cast—superbly—as the brash little night club M.C. In one of the big songs, 'Bewitched', Larry had the leading middle-aged lady Mrs Prentiss Simpson driving the censor up the proscenium arch when she described her new lover with lines like:

> HE'S A LAUGH AND I LOVE IT
> BECAUSE THE LAUGH'S . . . ON ME . . .

The critical reaction to *Pal Joey* was varied. The important Brooks Atkinson praised the treatment but ended his notice with the words: 'Can you draw sweet water from a foul well?' Richard Watts Jr thought *Pal Joey* 'brilliant, sardonic and strikingly original'. It has been revived often and remains one of Rodgers and Hart's most rounded and effective works.

Larry Hart was slipping rapidly into his own personal oblivion. Rodgers approached him about writing the lyrics for *Oklahoma* but Larry said 'No'. Rightly, I think, for beautiful as the show turned out to be, it was not the kind of folksy subject that would have been, lyrically, his cup of tea. He gave his blessing to Rodgers' projected collaboration with Hammerstein. But now he began to skid at speed, and friends would cross the road rather than greet the unkempt, reeling figure. His companions were the friends of the sinister Doc Bender and it was always Larry who picked up the tab. His real friends did arrange for a certain William Kron to manage his business affairs and put a brake on the spending. Kron must have done well for somebody. He was, it transpired, amply provided for in Larry's will.

Larry's mother died and he was completely alone. Herb Fields and Dick Rodgers thought that work could be the answer but some discussion was needed about how to pin him down to it. A revival, perhaps? Of *A Connecticut Yankee*, brought up to wartime date and with a few more songs? Larry's favourite lady Vivienne Segal would star. He had asked his brother Teddy only a short time ago, 'How would you like Vivienne Segal for a sister-in-law?' Teddy had been delighted but Miss Segal, much as she admired the little genius, didn't love him. He didn't measure up as a husband but he could write songs for her, and the new *Connecticut Yankee* had one of Larry's top lyrics. It was to be his last . . . the title, 'To keep my love alive' . . .

> I MARRIED MANY MEN, A TON OF THEM
> BUT STILL I WAS UNTRUE TO NONE OF THEM
> BECAUSE I BUMPED OFF EV'RY ONE OF THEM
> TO KEEP MY LOVE ALIVE . . .

Throughout the preparation for *A Connecticut Yankee* Larry had remained on the wagon, almost as though he were trying to rise to a challenge. *Oklahoma* was a smash hit—lyrics by Oscar Hammerstein, music by Richard Rodgers . . . of Rodgers and Hart . . . The thoughts that must have tortured him every time he came near the St James's Theatre. The revival opened in Philadelphia . . . *'I'll go to hell for ya—or Philadelphia'* . . . and Larry began drinking and losing, as he always did, his overcoat. A despairing, friendless, top-coatless alcoholic, paraded round the bars in pneumonia weather by a clutch of cronies who wanted nothing of him but the paper in his wallet. He attended the opening of *A Connecticut Yankee* in New York at the Martin Beck Theatre. Everyone tried to keep him away—from his own first night. His collaborator who had branched away from him on a road to triumphs and glories of which Larry would not be part detailed two men to watch him and see that he didn't enter the auditorium. Larry evaded them and stood at the back. When Vivienne Segal began her number he joined in noisily and, by Dick Rodgers' correct enough instruction, was bundled out of the theatre.

Teddy Hart's wife got him into a taxi and home to her apartment. There she settled him on a sofa and went to pick up Teddy after his show. When they got back Larry was sleeping and they left him and went to bed. During the night he got up and went home where he was found two days later—why so long?—in a coma. Dick and Dorothy Rodgers, Teddy Hart and his wife, William Kron and, inevitably, Doc Bender waited outside his room at the hospital. The date was November 22nd 1943. There was a practice air-raid alert and the lights went out suddenly. When they came on again a few moments later a doctor was there to tell them that Larry Hart was dead. He was forty-eight.

It isn't easy to believe that this swell and witty little man who could write so sensitively, with such flair and originality and had such success with his writings, was unable to draw happiness, satisfaction, the comfort of fulfilment from the knowledge that he could make the world sing ... and laugh ... and revel in a new sophistication, a new way with a love song, new rhyming patterns. Philip Leavitt, who had introduced Rodgers to Hart, summed up his contribution: 'I should say that Larry Hart is one of the great geniuses of lyric writing. Nobody has approached him before or since.'

Why wasn't that enough for him? Another question ... Why, when Dick Rodgers was cushioned in home comfort, could just a little of it not have come the way of Larry Hart? A presence in his life, a steadying presence, might have done so much. 'He outdid the handsomest men at the Hollywood party,' said the lady, 'with his charm and personality.' And he went home alone. Of course, if you can't cosy up to a lady it doesn't follow you have to do it to a bottle. Whether or not they gave him satisfaction, the verses are there.

'They just ring like pure gold,' said Agnes de Mille, who choreographed so brilliantly the *Oklahoma* for which he didn't write the lyrics.

There is one lyric of Larry Hart's that, in the analysis of his complex story, refuses to leave me. It runs:

ONCE THERE WAS A THING CALLED SPRING
WHEN THE WORLD WAS WRITING VERSES
LIKE YOURS AND MINE;
ALL THE LADS AND GIRLS WOULD SING
WHEN WE SAT AT LITTLE TABLES AND DRANK MAY WINE;
NOW APRIL, MAY AND JUNE
ARE SADLY OUT OF TUNE . . .
LIFE HAS STUCK THE PIN IN THE BALLOON . . .

SPRING IS HERE,
WHY DOESN'T MY HEART GO DANCING?
SPRING IS HERE,
WHY ISN'T THE WALTZ ENTRANCING?
NO DESIRE, NO AMBITION LEADS ME . . .
MAYBE IT'S BECAUSE NOBODY NEEDS ME . . .
SPRING IS HERE,
WHY DOESN'T THE BREEZE DELIGHT ME?
STARS APPEAR,
WHY DOESN'T THE NIGHT INVITE ME?
MUST BE IT'S BECAUSE NOBODY LOVES ME . . .
SPRING IS HERE, I HEAR!

It may be that the last five words of this lyric—they are so typically Larry Hart—tell the whole sadness. 'Spring is here . . . I hear.'

So much speculation over enigma. No one knows the deep inside of anybody. It could easily be that we are all wrong—biographers, friends . . . even relations. It could be that Lorenz Hart was simply a happy-as-Larry drunk with a touch of genius that puts him among the immortals. Fervently, I hope it was so.

NOËL and GERTIE
Pierrot and Columbine

Noël and Gertie in *Private Lives* at the Phoenix Theatre, London –
September 1930.

NOËL and GERTIE

This will not pretend to tell the individual full stories of Noël Coward and Gertrude Lawrence. I merely recall the overlaps in their lives; the partnership as it began, flourished, strained after dissolution but endured as friendship

Noël and Gertie. On the bills Noël gave her first placing. In the case of Spencer Tracy and Katharine Hepburn, Tracy came first, always. Somebody asked Tracy why. 'Why not?' he said. 'Well ...' somebody mumbled, '... after all, ladies first.' 'This', said Tracy, 'is a movie, not a goddamn lifeboat.' Of course, in the case of Coward and Lawrence, Noël had to be a touch more retiring because he wrote the plays in which they appeared together and the songs they sang. Euphony came into it in the world of Variety. 'Wilson, Kepple and Betty' wouldn't have sounded right in any other order. 'Johnstone and Layton' would have been unthinkable. I begin, though, with Gertie. So much has been told, and so often, about Noël that I put not only the lady first but the less known. (And how Gertie would have hated to admit that!)

Gertrud—without an 'e' at the end—Alexandra Dagmar Klasen was born, as you would not expect from the name, in Newington, London. At once there was a link with America. The date was Independence Day, July 4th 1898. Gertie claimed that it was 1901, perhaps because she would rather be a year younger than Noël than eighteen months older. His date of birth was December 16th 1899. Gertrud's father, Arthur Lawrence Klasen, was Danish. He was also a rather hammy, rather alcoholic bass singer who flourished at Christmas time as the Demon King in pantomime.

Noël Coward was born in Teddington, several cuts above Newington. His parents later ran a boarding house. Gertie, at the age of six, sang on a beach at Bognor (not, at that time, 'Regis') in a Pierrot competition and won a gold sovereign. Noël sang on a beach too, his Pierrots gave him a box of chocolates. Both went early on the stage. Gertie's mother had left the Demon King and remarried. She herself went into panto at Brixton, Babes in the Wood, and got Gertie in too, as one of Robin Hood's merry men. Gertie doubled as a robin red-breast. Noël had similar beginnings. Mother answered an advertisement, took him to an audition and la-la-ed while he sang because there was no piano. 'That,' said Noël, 'launched me into a children's fairy play called *The Goldfish* which was rather curious because in the first act we were all jolly, healthy children and in the second act we were all fish. I was Prince Mussel. The first line I ever said on the stage was "Crumbs, how exciting!"'

And so it proved to be. Gertie's mother sent her to Italia Conti's school. Her new husband made little money and what he made was galloped away by horses who didn't gallop fast enough. She couldn't pay Miss Conti so Gertie had to help out on the staff. Coward was never a Conti boy but he got a job with a group from the school and travelled north with them. It was in the spring of 1912 that Noël met Gertie. 'Her face was far from pretty,' he remembers, 'but tremendously alive. She was very mondaine, carried a handbag with a powder puff and freely dabbed her generously turned-up nose. She confided to me that her name was Gertrude Lawrence but that I was to call her "Gertie" because everybody did. She then,' he recalls, 'gave me an orange and told me a few mildly dirty stories and I loved her from then onwards.'

Noël and Gertie remained friends and Noël, who had begun writing at ten, promised one day to create a play for her. In the meantime, his own career forged ahead under the great light comedian Charles Hawtrey. For a girl, it was not as easy. Gertie had cards printed that read 'Little Gertie Lawrence, Child Actress and Danseuse', but they didn't help a lot. Little Gertie however, became bigger Gertie and André Charlot, the man who brought us intimate revue, employed her as general understudy in *Cheep*. She began to pick up the tricks of the stage trade. She also picked up the stage manager, a Mr Howley, married him, bore him a daughter and left him. It was in cabaret at Murray's Club that Gertie came spectacularly to notice. The noticers were often noble, sometimes royal. Philip Astley fell in love with her and taught her to be a socialite. She learned quickly how to dress, speak and behave in high company and, significantly, how to spend money. In 1923, she was back with Charlot at the Duke of York's in *London Calling*, so entitled in celebration of a recent invention known as 'the wireless'. Noël wrote half the material and appeared in it with Gertie. The choreography was by a new American star named Fred Astaire who was appearing in London in *Stop Flirting*. Gertie sang Noël's first hit song to a doll. 'Parisian Pierrot' was perhaps a grateful hark-back to the troupe who had rewarded him on the beach—though on second thoughts it probably wasn't, because this French pierrot's spirits were 'zero'.

The press loved Gertie in *London Calling* but said of Noël: 'He can't compose and should sing only for his friends' amazement.' One paper called him 'the most promising amateur in the West End'. We theatre folk need to be made of stern stuff. Noël was, even when Charlot left him playing in London and took Gertie with Bea Lillie and Jack Buchanan off to New York. *Charlot's London Revue of 1924* was a smash hit on Broadway, Jack Buchanan receiving rave reviews for the very numbers Noël had had trouble in putting over in London. On their return to England, Charlot presented a midnight matinée at which thirty-odd stars were photographed in a stage group. Noël was present and in the picture and quite unabashed—with reason, since he had left Charlot and taken London town in his own straight drama, *The Vortex*.

Gertie continued with revue and her association with Noël

moved in and out of focus like the picture when you fiddle with the lens on a projector. One sketch she played with Bea Lillie, *Fallen Babies*, was a skit on Noël's *Fallen Angels*. When Gertie arrived in New York to open in the Charlot 1926 revue, Noël was already on Broadway in *The Vortex*. Gertie had never earned so much—$2,500 a week, nor spent so much—$2,500 plus. Appropriately, she was also singing another Coward song. He had written it for Alice Delysia but, lyrically it might have been a hymn to Gertie:

POOR LITTLE RICH GIRL . . .
YOU'RE WEAVING LIFE INTO A MAD JAZZ PATTERN . . .
POOR LITTLE RICH GIRL . . .
BETTER BEWARE, BETTER TAKE CARE . . .
POOR LITTLE RICH GIRL . . .
DON'T DROP A STITCH TOO SOON!

It was *Oh, Kay!*, with book by Guy Bolton and P. G. Wodehouse, and music and lyrics by the Gershwins, that established Gertie as a solo star. The year was 1927, the place Broadway. Gertie had fallen for a Wall Street banker. The news reached Philip Astley in England and, suitably galvanized, he shot over to New York to propose marriage. Gertie turned him down. When she went to London in *Oh, Kay!* the banker, no doubt apprehensive about propinquity, shot over to London to propose and Gertie said 'Yes'—though in fact the matter never came to a head. Gertie's only and lasting love was the theatre, yet like many of us she failed to realize that when the lights are dimmed at the end of a performance there is no beloved less able to offer anything in return.

Gertie's socializing took her dangerously near to snobbery. Once, to Noël, she was unwise enough to mention that she was off to the South of France because she 'couldn't bear to winter in London'. Noël's reply was, 'Of course not, dear. Not after those childhood days you spent in sun-drenched Clapham.'

Gertie had been longing to make the step from the musical to the straight theatre. She managed it at last in *By Candle Light* opposite a promising newcomer named Leslie Howard. The play opened in New York in September 1929. Noël's wire read: LEGITIMATE AT LAST STOP WON'T MOTHER BE PLEASED. 1929 also brought the Wall Street crash and the consequent crash of Gertie's banker. She sent to remind Noël of his promise to write something for her. But Fanny Holtzman, her lawyer and manager, said: 'Keep working, stop hoping,' so she signed with Charlot again for revue. By the next post a script arrived from Noël. As he recalled the matter:

'I had always wanted to write a play for Gertie . . . Her contract with Charlot was up. She sent me a wire saying CONTRACT WITH CHARLOT UP WHAT ABOUT IT—or something. I wrote *Private Lives* in Shanghai, in the Cathay Hotel . . . very quickly . . . and posted it off. I had a telegram saying HAVE READ SCRIPT NOTHING WRONG THAT CAN'T BE FIXED. I wired back THE ONLY THING THAT'S GOING TO BE FIXED WILL BE YOUR PERFORMANCE. She later got out of that by pretending that what she meant was her contract with Charlot . . .'

Coward dissolved into a mixture of laughter and tears as he added: 'It . . . didn't ring true . . .!'

Private Lives was a landmark in the public lives of both Noël and Gertie. They recorded two scenes. We youngers played and played both sides of the twelve-inch 78 on our portable gramophones after seeing the production, and came to know every classic line and every note of the songs, some of which Gertie quite often didn't quite make.

Private Lives opened at—in fact, opened—the new Phoenix Theatre in September of 1930. It was an immediate hit in London and, within no time at all, in New York. Gertie, who also received a cut in the managerial profits, should have been able to bring herself well out of the red. But Noël closed after three months in each city. He was far more a stage personality than an actor and lacked that vital part of an actor's equipment that enables him to support a long run without boredom. Gertie got bored too, but from mere lack of discipline. For six brief months she poured pounds and dollars by the sack into her bank account—and out of it. Of her onstage undiscipline Noël said:

'She is potentially capable of anything and everything. She can be gay, sad, witty, tragic, funny and touching. She can play a scene one night with perfect subtlety and restraint and the next with such obviousness and over-emphasis that your senses reel. She has in abundance every theatrical essential but one: critical faculty. But for this tantalizing lack of discrimination she could, I believe, be the greatest actress alive in the theatre today.'

Gertie's extravagance continued. She sent her daughter to Roedean. She set up a flower shop in partnership with two friends but, since she gave credit where none was due and sent blooms by the bucket-load to herself, the economics wilted. Fanny Holtzman helped her into movies, but she never succeeded in making the celluloid grade. Fanny promoted *Nymph Errant* for Gertie in London, asking Noël to write the words and music. Noël was a touch rude in his refusal, announcing that he didn't see why he should be at Miss Lawrence's beck and call. So Fanny approached Cole Porter who proceeded to create, he thought, one of his best scores. 'Experiment' was one of the songs. For another, Cole locked himself away for an entire weekend with a medical dictionary and produced 'The Physician'. He produced 'Solomon' which Miss Elizabeth Welch made her very own.

Agnes de Mille, who would later arrange the stunning dance routines for *Oklahoma*, choreographed *Nymph Errant*, but Gertie was inclined to take steps of her own. She drove the designer, brilliant Doris Zinkeisen, mad by going into dresses of her own when the spirit moved her. She continued to fascinate the opposite sex—Agnes de Mille, perhaps in choreographic despair, called her 'a coquette par excellence'. In the summer of 1932, the escorting male was Douglas Fairbanks Junior.

The gay social round continued. 'I've taken a house in Berkeley Square,' said Gertie to Bea Lillie who responded with: 'Well, dear, you'll just have to put it back again, won't you?' At last those exigent authorities, the Inland Revenues of Great Britain and America, caught up with Gertie. Never tempted to under-dramatize, Gertie wrote:

> When I came out of the court I had nothing but the clothes I stood in. My cars, my apartment, my jewels, even some of my clothes were seized. Dorothy, my faithful maid, Mack, my dog, and I stood on the pavement outside the house. We had literally not a roof to crawl under. No money and no credit . . .

My agents at that time were a firm called O'Bryen, Linnet and Dunfee. Bill O'Bryen introduced Gertie to Bill Linnit who lent her his chambers in Albany, a roof not to be sneezed at, if you can sneeze at a roof.

From Albany, Gertie moved under Noël's more commodious tileage, Goldenhurst, a sixteenth-century farmhouse overlooking the Romney Marshes, and began to rehearse with him the one-act plays that would open at the Phoenix Theatre in January of 1936 under the title *Tonight at 8.30*. At first there were three plays, then six, which they played in repertory . . . then, finally, nine. One of the most popular was *Red Peppers*, in which they portrayed a seedy vaudeville twosome.

In the case of *Tonight at 8.30* Noël would once again play only a limited run—and this time despite the constant changes of character. One hundred and fifty performances would be the most he would allow himself, and the rest of the company, all of whom had to accept the reality that if you were in a smash hit with Noël you wouldn't run anyway. He had the usual trouble keeping the mercurial Gertie within bounds. They even came, Noël admitted, to blows . . . or a blow.

'I once hit her lightly,' he said, '. . . with a telescope while we were rehearsing the dance for *Red Peppers*. She turned on me with a wounded cry that Bernhardt would have envied and said "you struck me!" Whereupon we both laughed so much that we had to stop the rehearsal.'

Noël had no telescope in another of the plays, he merely exchanged words with Gertie then wired his manager, John C. Wilson, in New York: EVERYTHING LOVELY STOP CRACKING ROW WITH GERTIE OVER HANDS ACROSS THE SEA LASTING SEVEN MINUTES STOP HER PERFORMANCE EXQUISITE EVER SINCE.

Later, in mock fury, he cabled Wilson: VERY SORRY TO FIND MY ENGAGEMENTS WILL NOT PERMIT ME APPEAR UNDER YOUR BANNER IN AMERICA UNLESS I GET A FURTHER FIFTY EIGHT PER CENT OF THE GROSS FOR ARDUOUS TASK RESTRAINING MISS LAWRENCE FROM BEING GROCK, BEATRICE LILLIE, THEDA BARA, MARY PICKFORD AND BERT LAHR ALL AT ONCE.

Hands Across the Sea was recalled by Lord Louis Mountbatten at Noël's Seventieth Birthday Dinner at the Savoy:

'In 1936, in a burst of unusual generosity, Noël sent me half a dozen complimentary tickets for *Tonight at 8.30*. When we went in a party the second play was *Hands Across the Sea* and we saw with rising horror and indignation that it was just a travesty of our own lives. Gertrude Lawrence playing Lady Maureen Gilpin was unmistakably Edwina. I thought it was really rather funny, I laughed quite a bit. But Noël Coward as Commander Peter Gilpin was a disgrace and what annoyed me even more was that Edwina kept laughing.'

Another of the *Tonight at 8.30* pieces was the nostalgic *Shadow Play*. To convey Gertie's onstage magic if you never saw her is lamentably hard, particularly in the case of her singing. In *Shadow Play* I heard her damage one song seriously by sliding only a demi-semitone off a top note. A week later she was bang on. Was she more often bang on than bang off?—who knew unless you were in the shadows? The point is that nobody minded, even when she slid for the record. The magic was not aural alone. Now, of course, in the era of synthetic performance she would simply have a few goes at these top notes on a separate bit of tape and the engineers would do a repair job. Since Gertie recorded in earlier days posterity must take the flat with the smooth.

Before Gertie left England to open on Broadway in the plays she bought a house in Buckinghamshire. Bill O'Bryen, who was now her British agent, went white when he heard about it, which took a bit of doing because Bill was a ruddy-faced character. He cabled his remonstrances. Gertie cabled back: WIRE COST OF PUTTING IN SWIMMING POOL. I don't recall whether or not she took that plunge but it would have made a splashing hole in her financial cut from the Broadway production of *Tonight at 8.30*. Brooks Atkinson didn't endear himself to Noël in his notice:

> Although Mr Coward has written his miniatures with skill and acts them admirably, it is Miss Lawrence's triumph and further proof that one who seemed not long ago to be merely an amusing hoyden has now become a brilliant actress.

The *Tonight at 8.30* plays—the overall title was varied to suit the opening times—were the last writings Noël made for Gertie. They came back to London to see the Coronation procession but when Gertie returned to New York she travelled alone and to stay. Their friendship continued, and the Master's advice, when asked for, was freely given. Gertie took to journeying to, and appearing at, the Cape Playhouse in Denver, Massachusetts, whose Director, Richard Aldrich, fell under her spell. Gertie didn't resist for long, marrying him in July 1940. Noël, when he heard the news, said he thought she must have mistaken him for a member of the wealthy Winthrop Aldrich family. He des-

The 'Red Peppers' – Phoenix Theatre, January, 1936.

patched a cable: DEAR MRS ALDRICH AT LAST YOU ARE DEFLOWERED—which didn't say a lot for her first husband, Mr Howley—ON THIS AND EVERY OTHER DAY I LOVE YOU NOËL COWARD. There was pretty general surprise at the marriage. What did Mr Aldrich have that the theatre didn't? To a film producer who wished her happiness, Gertie made a strange reply: 'Happy or not, I need roots and he is a very firm root.'

In wartime, Gertie threw herself into the part of a worker for the war effort and played it up to the dramatic hilt. She and Noël were on the board of the British Actors' Orphanage and she superintended the evacuation to America of many a child. Typically, she spoiled them out of recognition and they didn't want to go home.

Moss Hart, the playwright—or half a playwright—now came into Gertie's life. He had written success after success with George S. Kaufmann, but this dependence upon another was having a lowering effect, especially since Kaufmann, when asked who contributed what in this partnership, had said: 'I'm the guy that walks up and down.' Hart consulted a psychiatrist, whose first invitation to lie down may well have caused a spasm in the unhappy collaborator. Said the shrink, 'Write something on your own, good or bad no matter, write it!' On the way home, Hart asked himself, 'What do I know enough about to write about?' 'Psychiatry,' he answered himself. He wrote the book of *Lady in the Dark*. Kurt Weill set to music lyrics by Ira Gershwin.

Gertie drove them up every wall around Broadway before she signed. Noël had to be asked, she insisted. Noël commiserated with Moss Hart. 'But she said yes!' said Hart. Noël's cryptic reply was, 'That's what I mean.' *Lady in the Dark* opened at the Alvin Theatre in January of 1941 and was a tremendous success. It had a three-year run on Broadway but was never played in London (impresarios, please note. But also note that we now have no Miss Lawrence). Gertie was at the top of her form. One critic commented: 'Vitamins should take Gertrude Lawrence.'

When America entered the war at the end of 1941 Gertie donned uniform, posed in it looking like Hedda Gabler as Gertrude Lawrence and, later, did her full travel stint giving troop concerts. In Honolulu she played Elvira in Noël's *Blithe Spirit*, though Noël was not too happy at not having been consulted over this. Their last appearance on a stage together happened in 1947. Gertie was starring in a revival of *Tonight at 8.30* and had reached San Francisco. Her co-star, Noël's friend Graham Payn, was taken ill and the Master stepped in. It was perhaps a pity that he stepped out again. When the plays reached Broadway the critics were cooler to Gertie and Graham than they had been to Noël and Gertie. Of the plays, one wrote: 'It is not that they have mellowed with age like wine but that they have puckered and wrinkled like cocoa . . .'

Gertie Lawrence, in common with some of the rest of us, discovered that the world had begun to pucker. Her last London appearance, at the Aldwych Theatre in Daphne du Maurier's *September Tide*, called for her to make an omelette on stage—mix it, not cook it, the director knew his Gertie. But . . . Miss Gertrude Lawrence making an omelette with powdered egg? During her American war work she could well have superintended the packing of it and the sending as part of a 'bundle for Britain'. The press were reverent but not ecstatic about her return, and there was no longer a throng of admirers at the stage door to see her. It was a brave new post-war world of 'I'm-as-good-as-you' in which, *ipso facto*, magic had no place. She expected her young leading man to escort her to supper but he was otherwise engaged with another—younger—member of the cast. Gertie's thoughts were less benign than those she would express when she sang:

HELLO, YOUNG LOVERS, WHOEVER YOU ARE . . .
ALL MY GOOD WISHES GO WITH YOU TONIGHT . . .

The song is, of course, from *The King and I*, Gertie's last show. She had acquired, through the redoubtable Miss Holtzman, the rights of Margaret Landon's 1944 best seller *Anna and the King of Siam*. Rodgers and Hammerstein were commissioned to write the score, Rodgers cleverly apportioning the songs so that Gertie's voice would not be overtaxed in the high register. Fanny Holtzman had the idea that Noël should play the King. It would have been fascinating—would the Master have shaved his head? One thing is certain, Noël would have abdicated after three months and he knew it. Like Caesar, he declined the crown. Gertie was happy to sign for a long run but would never complete it. Failing health began, even during rehearsals, to pull her away from her one love, the theatre.

The King and I opened superbly on March 29th 1951. 'An original and beautiful excursion into the rich splendours of the Far East,' said Brooks Atkinson. 'A show of a thousand delights', wrote Richard Watts, 'with the magic of Gertrude Lawrence.' The director, John Van Druten, recorded:

> Her comedy in the part was gentler, Victorian, almost evasive and her touch on the sweeter and more personal notes was stronger and surer. Her radiance was there and her star quality indefinable but intensely vivid. She had a power to move not only the audience but the very boards of the stage as she stepped on them.

Gertie's appearances in *The King and I* became fewer as the year 1952 progressed. Nobody suspected that she was suffering from cancer. She died on September 6th. The theatre lights—on Broadway and, at theatre time, in London—were dimmed for one minute. In tribute, Noël said:

> 'For me, the years are full of memories of her, both on the stage and off it. Among these memories I cannot find one that is mean or unkind or to be regretted. I have seen her act more brilliantly and exquisitely than anyone else I know. I have also seen her overact, badly. I have heard her sing truly and sweetly and I have also heard her sing off key. I've been angry with her

Gertie with Yul Brynner in her last show, *The King and I*. It opened in
Broadway in March, 1951 – eighteen months before her death.

one minute and at her feet the next but I have never at any time had any reason to question her loyalty or mistrust her generous, loving heart. The last time I saw her was in April. We lunched together at her house in New York and I promised to write a play for her to play in in England next year. Almost the last words she said to me were "I want to come home". I wish so very deeply that she had come home and that I could have seen her just once more playing in a play of mine for no one I've ever known, however brilliant and however gifted, has contributed quite what she contributed to my work. Her quality was, to me, unique, and her magic imperishable.'

Noël went on to expected peaks. Then there was hiatus. After being, for a time, an anachronism he enjoyed revival, knighthood and the status of a living legend until his death in 1973.

Gertie never did, to my knowledge, appear in Shakespeare but she chose a quotation from the Bard as the title of her autobiography. It may have been Noël who chose it, since he was fond of using Shakespearean titles—*This Happy Breed, Present Laughter, Sigh No More* . . . Gertie as Beatrice in *Much Ado About Nothing* would, in fact, have made a match for Noël Coward's Benedick, had he been an actor in the real sense. When asked about her origins, Beatrice says: 'A star danced, and under that I was born.' *A Star Danced* is the title Gertie settled for.

Gertrude Lawrence, born under a dancing star, her talent dancing, briefly, for our delight . . . How lucky for us, and for the theatre, that Noël was around to partner her and to occupy at least a little of her dance programme.

JUDY GARLAND
Rainbows

Judy in the costume of the early 1900's in *Meet me in St. Louis*.

JUDY GARLAND

Judy Garland was born Frances Ethel Gumm. Not in a trunk, not in Pocatella, Idaho, but in Grand Rapids, Minnesota.

Nobody chased rainbows like Judy. She came from a long line of rainbow chasers. Her mother Ethel Milne was one, and so was her mother before her. The rainbow proved to be a mirage for grandma; Ethel wound up thumping a piano in a movie house but she wasn't going to admit defeat. She met Frank Gumm, a fun-loving Irishman from Tennessee who sang tenor. They married and went on the halls as 'Jack and Virginia Lee—Sweet Southern Singers'.

The Gumms soon had two daughters, Virginia and Susie. By now, Frank Gumm owned a movie house in Grand Rapids Minnesota but life there wasn't grand enough, or rapid enough, for Ethel Gumm. A third daughter came along in June 1922. They were so certain it would be a boy they got the local newspaper to announce the birth of 'Francis Gumm Jr.'. By the time the paper went to press it was 'Frances'.

Jimmy and Susie were eight and five, respectively, when mother had them singing and hoofing it on the stage at Frank's movie house while the projectionist went out for a prohibited beer. Frances sat on her grandmother's knee in the front row. She whimpered and granny perched her on the side of the stage. 'Get her off!' yelled Ethel, banging away at the pit piano. Frances was already toddling to stage centre and getting applause for being unsteady on her pins. 'Sing!' shouted the audience and she gave them 'Jingle bells'. She stopped the show. Mother was surprised but delighted. Baby Frances was happy, not dreaming what was to follow, but Frank Gumm knew and was in despair. Ethel made him sell his movie house, packed the family into the jalopy and headed for the Golden City of Hollywood.

Ethel pushed her offspring into any crummy vaudeville date she could get on the way in case a talent scout might be scouting, even a crummy talent scout. She produced the act, played the piano, and came on at the end to ruin it. Father drove the jalopy and handled what business there was. You could say the Gumm family was really in full cry after rainbows. Speaking of rainbows, it occurs here that Judy's companions on that trip to see the *Wizard of Oz* were a scarecrow without a brain, a tin man without a heart and a frightened lion. And the Wizard, when she found him, was a phoney. As things were going to turn out Judy was good casting.

The Gumms hit Hollywood but Hollywood failed to react. Frank bought a movie house eighty miles north of Los Angeles. He did well at it and bought two more ... but Ethel went on chasing rainbows with the three girls. Then she left Jimmy and Susie at home and concentrated on Frances, bowling her around like a hoop from hotel to hotel. When the child became fretful, Ethel packed a bag, told her she was leaving and went out locking the door of the hotel room behind her. She was gone for hours. When she came back she found Frances hysterical and willing to agree to anything to avoid a repetition of the punishment.

Frank Gumm's modest personal rainbow was a simple family life. At one point he nearly achieved it. He sold his three cinemas and bought one nearer to Ethel's rainbow—Hollywood. With the balance he bought a house. The girls went to Miss Lawton's School for Professional Students. It was here that Frances met Mickey Rooney. Mickey was able to laugh her out of sadness caused by rows at home, but he never dated her. It was glamorous pupils like Lana Turner and Ava Gardner he gave his attention to. He even took to marrying them later in quite a big way. He left Frances Gumm nursing an enormous inferiority feeling about her looks.

The Gumm Sisters played at the Chicago World's Fair. They were horrified to find that they were billed as 'The Glum Sisters', and made an understandable fuss. George Jessel, who was topping the bill, said he didn't think 'Gumm' was much better than 'Glum'. There was a critic backstage at the time named Robert Garland. 'What about "Garland"?' said Jessel. Up they went as 'The Garland Sisters'. For a first name Frances begged to be called after her favourite song. Hoagy Carmichael had written it, and, all unknowing, dubbed her 'Judy'.

It was during a four-week engagement at Lake Tahoe that an agent named Al Rosen saw and heard Judy and decided to take ten per cent of her under his wing. He got a Jewish friend who was a cantor to work on her voice. He may well have been instrumental in developing the unique 'from-the-heart' quality that was to stamp her singing. Rosen introduced Judy to Roger Edens who coached her and accompanied her when, at last, she sang for the great and dreaded Louis B. Mayer. At the end of the song Mayer walked out in silence. He was silent for two weeks, then he signed Judy.

Everybody who wanted to remain anybody in Hollywood licked the boots of Louis B. Mayer. He had immigrated from Poland and had come up by way of scrap metal. Even Hippocrates didn't stand a chance. Because Judy was overweight Mayer ordered the studio doctor to prescribe pituitary pills. The pituitary gland, I'm told on good authority, is one gland you don't tangle with, especially when dealing with a twelve-year-old girl. She was prescribed stimulants to keep her sparkling before the cameras for a twelve-hour day and tranquillizers to bring her sleep. She was made to live on chicken soup and when she tried to sneak something more substantial at the canteen was reported by Mayer's private Gestapo. 'No' was a word incomprehensible to Mayer. God knows what poor Judy said when she was alone with him in his huge office. Young girls were Mayer's rainbows but he chased them with a degree of certainty. It was said he never promised stardom if a girl succumbed but promised to destroy her if she didn't. This, I suppose, is called 'hedging your rainbows'. Nobody dared to talk, of course, and it is quite likely that Mayer's bedridden wife never heard of these forays.

The studio had Judy performing in public from time to time to gain experience. She appeared at parties given by the stars. Clark Gable threw one and Judy popped up out of a cake to sing 'Dear Mr Gable'. Years later, on his birthday, he said to Judy: 'I thought there was going to be a cake and you'd come out of it and sing that goddamn song.'

Three months after she had been signed away to MGM, still not having appeared before the cameras, Judy was singing on the Al Jolson radio programme when her father died of meningitis. She locked herself in a bathroom for fourteen hours crying and vomiting and crying again. Then Ethel packed her off to the studio where Louis B. Mayer told her: 'From now on I'll be your father.' It was a favourite line of his. From her loving Irish Dad to this paternally-spoken weirdie was quite a shift for Judy. For sixteen years she would never make a move Mayer didn't dictate. Her screen appearances, her off-screen life ... her dates, her marriages, her divorces ... all were ordered, or disordered, by the man who had risen from scrap-metal to scrap-stars. Ringmaster Mayer was in full regalia. The circus began.

Judy's first movie was in the nature of a screen test. It was a short in which she countered Deanna Durbin, Deanna singing sweet, Judy swinging. She sang 'Dear Mr Gable', because Mayer liked it, in a movie that was made in '36, released in '37 and called *Broadway Melody of 1938*. The *New York Times* referred to her as 'Metro's answer to Deanna Durbin'. The *Hollywood Reporter* said: 'The sensational work of young Judy Garland causes wonder as to why she has been kept under wraps these many months...'

But Judy was far from amassing any degree of confidence. At home she was called 'Pudge' or sometimes 'Monkey'. Mayer called her 'My little hunch-back'—she was only five feet two but didn't need reminding. No such thing as puppy fat was allowed for at MGM, the studio knowing better than nature. The diet pills made her slimmer but ever more wakeful. She was fourteen when the MGM doctor put her on seconals.

Soon Judy was working on more than one film at once. In *Thoroughbreds Don't Cry* she was on the screen for the first time with Mickey Rooney, who received $5000 a week against Judy's $150. In *Everybody Sing* the publicist announced: 'Adorable Judy Garland zooms to stardom on wings of song.' But she didn't zoom to star salary. Her agent Al Rosen broached the matter but Mayer said 'No' and Rosen didn't argue. The studio did agree to pay Ethel $200 a week. This of course put her on the MGM payroll, right under Mayer's thumb.

Mayer wanted Shirley Temple for *The Wizard of Oz* but luckily, not only for Judy but for all of us, Fox wouldn't release her. The part was a dream child of eleven. Judy was sixteen and now quite buxom. The fasting was stepped up, her bust strapped in, her teeth capped, and her hair dyed. Judy had always been deeply ashamed of her hair. They told her that, even dyed, it looked awful, and stuck a wig on it. She must have faced the cameras feeling every restricted inch a nightmare child.

For playing Dorothy in *The Wizard of Oz*, Judy Garland received $350 a week, in those days £70. After paying Rosen, she—or Ethel—pocketed £63. Rosen made a bid to tackle Mayer again, but Mayer refused to see him. 'I have a friend,' he said to Ethel, 'who'd be a far better agent for your daughter.' The 'friend' was Frank Orsatti, known to be a supplier of ladies for the higher MGM executives, a sort of agent. Ethel said 'Yes' and Judy was handed over without her knowledge, without her agent's knowledge, the deal being done sub rosa, or sub Rosen. Orsatti fixed Judy's salary at a very modest $500, one tenth of Rooney's. Judy's success as Dorothy is part of the legend. One song Mayer cut from the completed film until somebody who knew persuaded him to put it back again. It was 'Somewhere over the rainbow'.

One dream that was just over the rainbow for Judy was her graduation from school. She had her dress ready months ahead. Mayer knew all about this, but Judy never made the dream. He sent her on a promotional tour with Rooney, doing five shows a

Judy with Mickey Rooney in *Strike up the Band* – made on pep pills.
'Most of the time we were hanging from the ceiling,' she said.

The sixteen-year-old Judy Garland in *The Wizard of Oz*. Her
companions are, left to right, Jack Haley, Bert Lahr and Ray Bolger.

day, with luncheons, dinners, benefits, broadcasts, and press interviews wedged in between. Not surprisingly she fainted in the wings and failed to appear at one performance—it was the first such failure but it was not to be the last.

Judy went back to studio work at full pitch. *Babes in Arms* was followed, within twelve hours, by *Andy Hardy Meets Debutante*. Then it was straight into *Strike up the Band* and *Babes on Broadway*. With hindsight you can in fact recall a kind of frenetic quality in the leading talents. Judy said:

> 'They had us working days and nights on end. They'd give us pep pills to keep us on our feet long after we were exhausted. Then they'd take us to the studio hospital and knock us cold with sleeping pills, Mickey sprawled on one bed and me on another. Then after four hours, they'd wake us up and give us the pep pills again so we could work another seventy-two hours in a row. Half the time we were hanging from the ceiling but it became a way of life for us...'

When Judy was seventeen Tyrone Power fell in love with her. He was handsome and a hot studio property—so she was attractive after all! Judy was over the moon and, of course, she fell too. Mayer put paid to the romance by threatening Power. On the rebound she fell in love with David Rose who was getting a divorce from Martha Raye. Mayer insisted they wait a year—a year in which he carefully arranged for Judy to make four pictures.

Judy, now eighteen and beginning actually to show a touch of independence, got herself a real agent and moved into her own apartment. But her work schedule staggered David Rose. Shooting now went on for sixteen, seventeen, eighteen hours a day. She had to be in make-up by six a.m. There were wardrobe fittings, stills sessions, song rehearsals, dance rehearsals ... dialogue to learn ... the press to be smiled at. When she became ravenous and ate something she put on a little weight, not fat, just weight, and at once was ordered back on diet pills. During these periods she lived on chicken soup and black coffee. Mayer liked to see bone structure, and I have a clear mental picture, as I expect we all have, of Judy's facial boniness in wartime movies. She was encouraged to smoke to keep her weight down and soon was managing eighty a day. And she dreamed of marrying David Rose, the man who had written the delightful escapist piece *Holiday for Strings*. She may have figured the strings were lucky.

In July 1941, aged nineteen, Judy eloped during a four-day break between pictures and married David. Mayer blew a gasket and cancelled the rest of her break, ordering her to the studio at once to begin *Babes on Broadway*.

In the middle of shooting, Judy Rose was thrilled to learn she was pregnant; David Rose, for reasons known to himself, was less thrilled. Ethel told Arthur Freed, who was producing the movie. Judy could finish this one without trouble, they decided, but she was due to go straight into *For Me and My Gal*. There were meetings which Judy was not invited to attend and the great gods of MGM decided that, in order not to interrupt the schedule, Mrs Rose should undergo an abortion. Incredibly, Judy agreed. David's lack of enthusiasm may have had something to do with it, it seemed to her nobody was on her side. Such goings-on were illegal at the time but MGM was well above the law. Mayer announced that Judy needed a tonsillectomy and had the studio doctor perform the other operation. Within four days she was back at work, recording songs for the movie she had just made about the young in entertainment.

Understandably perhaps, Judy began to harden a little in her feelings about men, but she continued to need love with a kind of desperation. She became alarmingly thin. The diet pills were stopped but the inevitable withdrawal symptoms moved in. A critic wrote of *For Me and My Gal*: 'Judy looked thin and frail throughout but she seems to have developed enormously as an actress since *Babes on Broadway*.' So that's how you learn! She was now one of the ten top box office attractions in films and earning a mint for MGM. She was also paying secret visits to a psychiatrist. When you begin this kind of thing in America—

perhaps elsewhere?—you need to have a private and accessible Fort Knox. She and David Rose were divorced in February 1943, after little more than eighteen months of marriage.

Judy was earning huge sums now, but huge sums were also going out, and not only on psychiatry. Ethel and her new husband Bill Gilmore were investing her money as unwisely as could be and putting nothing aside for tax. With Busby Berkeley, who had directed her in *For Me and My Gal* and *Ziegfeld Girl*, Judy began work on *Girl Crazy*. Berkeley's perfectionism now proved to be too much for her tired body and she had him replaced; poor Buzz didn't know what hit him. It was Judy's first brush with a director, but she still delivered the goods. All the time the bills were piling up. Judy was soon to lose the house she had bought with David Rose—the house in which Jean Harlow had died.

She sent Ethel to beg Mayer to let her rest in a clinic for six months. Mayer's reply was to cast her in *As Thousands Cheer*, then to send her on a personal appearance tour to promote the film. She gave her first concert, in the open air, to an audience of 36,000 fans. Despite her exhausted condition she seemed to draw energy from their adoration and went from strength to strength as the evening moved to a climax. The night moved to a climax too as she took vodka to speed up the action of her nembuthal sleeping pills. She managed to ring the psychiatrist before she collapsed. She now began five years of morning and evening sessions daily. Even Mayer had to take notice. He decided that what Judy needed was a husband, one who would be supremely loyal—to Mayer.

Judy didn't want to make *Meet Me in St Louis* but Mayer threatened to suspend her if she didn't. Incredibly, she was flat broke and had to agree. Vincente Minelli was directing. A kindly, sensitive man, he was also ambitious and, for this reason, very much a Mayer man. The fact that *Meet Me in St Louis* was second only to *Gone With the Wind* at the box office made Mayer a Minelli man. Minelli became a Judy man when he directed her in her first dramatic role in *Under the Clock*. She had always wanted to act and did it superbly. Nevertheless her next roll was in *The Harvey Girls*, another musical—with Minelli again.

Vincente Minelli and Judy Garland were married in June 1945. Judy was twenty-three. Mayer gave her away, in marriage, and contributed to their buying an enormous and enormously expensive house. This was another of Mayer's ploys: he liked to encourage the stars to overspend, thereby mortgaging them to the studio for life. Liza Minelli was born just nine months later, a Caesarean birth. Up and at work too soon, Judy collapsed in the street, and the doctor advised not rest, but complete retirement. He wasn't a Mayer man. Mayer's answer was to put Judy into three major musicals. Norman Zierold wrote:

> A jumpy, irritable Judy dragged herself to work with tears in her eyes and muted resistance deep in her heart. As the relentless drain on her energies continued, that resistance occasionally turned on the director. And the director, unfortunately, was sometimes her husband.

Judy filmed *The Pirate* for Minelli then entered a sanatorium. The studio suspended Judy and the Government chose this moment to sue her for past tax which Ethel had neglected to pay. *Easter Parade* is a great movie. When we see it it's as well we don't know that Judy got up out of bed to make it because she was broke. If we did, the knowledge would perhaps lend poignancy to her classic duet with Astaire, the 'Couple of Swells' on their beam ends.

The studio wanted to follow up the success of *Easter Parade* with another Astaire–Garland vehicle. Judy pleaded, unsuccessfully, with Mayer for a little time. She was now drinking because the spleeping pills were ceasing to take effect, and when she was absent from shooting one too many times on *The Barkleys of Broadway* Ginger Rogers was called in to replace her. Irving Berlin wanted Judy for his *Annie Get Your Gun*. She recorded her songs. At one session an underling delivered a note to her, which said, simply, 'Your services are no longer required.' It was Joe

Pasternak who probably saved Judy's life at this point by casting her, against fierce studio opposition, in a movie called *In the Good Old Summertime*.

Judy's marriage to Minelli came to an end in March 1949. She was advised by a doctor to spend six months in hospital. She made it three, then went into *Summer Stock*, again for Joe Pasternak. The studio ordered her to lose fifteen pounds before shooting. She lost seven and Pasternak settled for that. It went on again, came off, went on . . . her changes of weight are surprising and pathetic in the movie. After shooting had ended they decided to add a number, 'Get Happy'. In the two weeks that had passed Judy had lost twenty pounds, but Pasternak let it go. That 'Get Happy' is one of the best things on film, from Judy or anybody.

At long last Judy was released to spend time with her mother and daughter. She had been promised six months but after three weeks Mayer demanded her return to replace the pregnant June Allyson in *Royal Wedding*. It is believed Mayer hoped Judy would say 'No' and enable him to suspend her without payment. In fact, she tried to work but couldn't manage to keep to the schedule and Mayer was able to fire her, choosing to do so by telegram. Minelli came round to see her, concerned about Liza's presence in the house with her unstable mother. It is reported that Judy made several suicide attempts, though whether or not these were genuine attempts is questionable. On this occasion, after reading Mayer's telegram she locked herself in the bathroom and tried to cut her throat—surely a strange method to choose. She screamed and Minelli came at once. Was it a scream of pain or a cry for attention?

One fact was unquestionable: after sixteen years with MGM Judy was out. She had made, it has been estimated, 80 million dollars for them. The residuals would continue ad infinitum. When you see an MGM movie on television you may be assured they have picked up a fat fee. The actors pick up nothing. Though she had been well paid, latterly, Judy had never drawn a percentage of the gross receipts nor even of the profits. She had no golden handshakes, no pension. She was good and broke again. When she asked Mayer for a loan, he put it to Nicholas Schenck, Chairman of Loew's Incorporated, the Distribution side of MGM. Schenck refused. To save his own face Mayer gave Judy a personal loan equal to one week's salary. This may be the moment to recall the remark made by Sam Goldwyn, once a Mayer associate, in answer to someone who noticed the crowds of celebrities present at Mayer's funeral. 'Doesn't surprise me,' said Goldwyn. 'They want to be sure the son of a bitch is dead.'

The rest of the Garland story is too repetitiously tragic for me to dwell upon. Ethel, now divorced, was responsible for starting Judy on the concert tours that gave so much to us and took so much out of her—when she kept the dates. She made radio appearances. She met and married Sid Luft, who was a promoter with some flair. Their daughter, Lorna Luft, was born in December of 1952 but Judy's joy was offset by the death of her mother. For all that Ethel had done, Judy was devastated, and suffered a breakdown that lasted for two years. Then Sid Luft promoted, for Judy, a musical to end them all.

If any artist was going to win one of those Academy Awards for a length of celluloid, it would surely be Judy for *A Star is Born*. Luft had TV cameras set up in her bedroom at the hospital (she was back in one again) and she sat up in bed, happy in anticipation, fully made up to hear the names of the winners announced over the air ... The Best Actress Award went to Grace Kelly for *The Country Girl*, a performance that lit no fires for me personally. The effect on Judy must have been calamitous. Stubby Kaye was filming *Guys and Dolls* at the time, and told me that when the news broke Frank Sinatra grabbed him by the arm. 'Forget the commissariat for lunch,' he said. 'I've got a food basket, we can eat in the car.' 'Where are we going?' Stubby asked him. 'To see Judy,' said Frank. 'She'll need cheering up.' They were still in costume. Judy was overjoyed to receive a visit that day from Nathan Detroit and Nicely Nicely Johnson.

She continued with her concert tours—the Palace New York, the Palladium London. In 1961 she reduced her Carnegie Hall audience, it was written, to 'a loving, weeping, laughing, worshipping shambles'. She worked against the strictest medical advice. Those who complain about her apparent unprofessionalism, whether they be audience members or fellow actors, must be reminded of this. We were watching and squeezing the last drips of magic from a very sick woman who was performing to keep body and soul together, not her own alone but those of too many hangers-on. When she was on stage all seemed to be well. 'It's the only place,' she told us, 'where I feel equal ... and safe ...'

She was by now on the brink of a precipice. She had a son by Mr Luft, called Joey. Then there was estrangement and divorce. She married Mark Herron, a film extra, briefly and, even more briefly on a trip to London, Micky Deans. Quite often she didn't come through with the expected magic. 'I can't be spread so thin!' was the plea of a film character she played very close to herself. I saw her for the last time at the Dominion Theatre in London and she was quite superb, the magic working like a golden charm. She played her final concert in Copenhagen.

After abortive appearances at London's Talk Of The Town Judy died at a tiny mews house in Cadogan Lane on June 22nd 1969 from a combination of drugs, alcohol and sheer exhaustion. She was forty-seven. There was no money immediately available so her body waited for a whole year for burial. It was Liza, her daughter, who saw that she was appropriately laid to rest. So ended the saga of a girl who was starved of love. If she could have bought it at the MGM Commissariat someone would have told Mayer and he'd have made her spit it out. In fact, in essence, that's what he did. She grew up to have an insatiable appetite for love. Her last movie, *I Could Go On Singing*, was very much her story. Someone says of her in it: 'She gives more love than anyone. But she takes more love than anyone can possible give.' Thirty thousand people at a sitting gave and gave, and Judy was still in need. Stylish she was, but more than that she set a style. Hers was such a short, giving life. How lucky we were to be on the receiving end!

CARROLL GIBBONS
At the Savoy

Carroll Gibbons and the Savoy Hotel Orpheans in 1931. Carroll is at
the left hand piano

CARROLL GIBBONS

There were several sides to the piano style of Carroll Gibbons. The sprightly side . . . the lazily hiccuping triplets . . . the tempo change to single notes played with the right hand deep down in the bass—sometimes they carried the melody, or they might complement another instrument. Together they made up the sound that *was* the Savoy Hotel restaurant in the thirties and forties. The Gibbons style was unmistakable to millions who heard him on the air, bought and played his records or had the special privilege of dining and dancing at the Savoy in the golden years. Even in wartime when there was other metal about outside, there was pure gold within.

The tempo changes didn't, of course, happen during dancing at the Savoy; there all was smooth as silk. Carroll reserved them for his recordings. 'A bit of light and shade,' he may have said to himself, but it could be maddening. Suppose you liked dancing and not only liked dancing but liked the cosiness it could lead to . . . and couldn't afford the Savoy? I mean, it wasn't everyone in the thirties who could run to two or three pounds for dinner. You had to fall back on the Corner House and going home to listen to records. 'I've got the latest Carroll Gibbons,' you'd whisper. Better than etchings. During the slow bits you might get to first or second base very nicely while cheek-to-cheeking—only to have the ground swept from under you when Mr Gibbons changed tempo again.

Every bit as familiar to us was Carroll's style in speaking. The American accent, his drawling, unhurried introductions uttered on the radio . . . the slight hesitance, the hint of a stammer that had the ladies at his feet—or clustered about his piano. It was a deepish voice. To the ladies he would explain, 'I gargle with gravel.'

At the time I heard and saved up for and bought my first Carroll Gibbons record for two bob, I thought the song 'Stompin' at the Savoy' meant livin' it up at the hotel in the Strand, West Central London. Later, still extremely young, I actually dined there and wondered how anyone could speak of 'stompin'' to that supremely sophisticated music. All was made clear to me in the late thirties when I played on Broadway and trekked nightly to—and trucked at—the Savoy Ballroom in Harlem. So there were two Savoys! The one in London did go back—in name, anyway-to Gilbert and Sullivan so, stompin' or no stompin', you could say it had the edge.

To the playing and speaking style of Carroll Gibbons was added another facet. He was persuaded to sing. The odd vocal chorus to the accompaniment of his orchestra became a full vocal performance at the piano. Carroll would have been the last to lay claim to a singing voice but the ladies sighed—as Shakespeare had Jacques put it—'like furnace', and rushed to buy the records. We all bought them.

It wasn't until I went into song writing in the forties that I met Joe Brannelley, a friendly American who was connected with the publishing firm of Peter Maurice Music. In the twenties Joe played the banjo and was apparently something of a fixer—a finder of musicians. The Savoy Hotel Group, which included the Berkeley Hotel in Piccadilly, needed a sax player and Joe mentioned a fellow American named Rudy Vallee. Vallee was a college lad who had caused quite a stir among young females in America. He had copper-coloured curly hair and a voice that attracted even when singing through a megaphone. After spending a year at the University of Maine and singing 'Fill the stein for dear old Maine, shout till the rafters ring!' he left and went to Yale. Only in America would it be likely that a college man might interrupt his studies to travel the Vaudeville circuit with a band.

Rudy Vallee did. The band was the Yale Collegians. It isn't, I think, surprising that he didn't graduate until he was twenty-six. At twenty-three he was on the *Titanic*'s sister ship, the S.S. *Olympic*, bound for Southampton—and London, and a place in the Havana Band at the Savoy Hotel. The professors at Yale, once more, were left panting to instil knowledge while Rudy would blow into a sax and sing into a megaphone. Joe Brannelley met the boat train when it reached Victoria and noticed that Rudy had another lad with him. 'Name's Carroll Gibbons,' said Rudy, 'plays piano.' 'We don't need a pianist,' said Joe. 'He doesn't need you,' said Rudy, 'he's from the Boston Conservatory. Over here to study real music. Wait till you hear him though. It'll be up to you to talk him out of Chopin . . .' This was in 1924.

If only I had been a man about Mayfair at that time instead of a schoolboy about South East London I might have supped at the Berkeley—perhaps after seeing that American pair the Astaires who were taking the town at the Shaftesbury Theatre in *Stop Flirting*. There I might have danced to the music of the Boston Orchestra, all five of them: Howard Jacobs saxaphone, Reginald Pursglove violin . . . Joe Brannelley, banjo . . . Alec Ure drums . . . and, at the piano, a slight, white-faced youngster with black, bushy eyebrows. The Savoy Group men had heard Carroll Gibbons play and had persuaded him to play their kind of music. So . . . the boy from the Boston Conservatory was in the Boston Orchestra—it sounded right.

Carroll was born in Clinton, Massachusetts on January 4th, 1903 and was playing the piano in public at the age of ten. At that time Europe was the Mecca for classical music as America was the Mecca for jazz. It was strange—and lucky for us—that Carroll should come to London if not with classical music as his absolute goal, at least with a musically open mind, and should stay to play the kind of music that would normally attract an aspirant in the other direction. Soon he made a neat glissando down to the Strand where the Boston Orchestra stood in for the famous Savoy Orpheans and the Savoy Havana Band. In 1926 yet another group was formed, the Savoy Sylvians. Carroll was at the piano and in charge.

The most famous of the Savoy bands by the late twenties was the Orpheans. I had—or rather the relations I spent my summer holidays with had—a stack of records labelled 'Debroy Somers and the Savoy Hotel Orpheans'. Somers I would meet, too, in the forties. In 1927 he handed his Savoy baton to Carroll Gibbons. Carroll had met a fellow American named Jimmy Dyrenforth who, like Carroll, had decided to make his home in England, and they began writing songs together. Carroll took the Orpheans on a three-month tour of Germany then came back—not to lead them again at the Savoy but to become director of light music for H.M.V. A Rumanian ex-Minister of Agriculture was in London at that time. He hadn't yet starred for Charles B. Cochran in *Wake Up and Dream*, and *Bitter Sweet*, an even greater success for him, was still to come. The signs were good. He was handsome, had the currently popular European accent and a pleasant singing voice. When you are Director of Light Music for a major recording company why not record one of your own? In July of 1928 Carroll put on wax 'Garden in the rain' with George Metaxa singing.

Carroll's recordings for H.M.V. with the 'New Mayfair Orchestra' were popular enough but after little more than a year he handed over to Ray Noble and took off for Hollywood and the delights of working for Louis B. Mayer. Many stood these delights for quite a time. Carroll was back with us in 1931 and re-forming the Savoy Hotel Orpheans—with Howard Jacobs who also came from Massachusetts. In June 1932 Carroll assumed control and for more than two more decades would travel to and from that small turning off the Strand, the only street in London where you must drive on the right.

The golden years began and it seemed impossible they could ever end. There was a depression, they kept telling us. I can only say that I was at Drama School in the early thirties—on a scholarship, I couldn't have managed it otherwise—and I wasn't depressed. I don't know why. Quite a few of us lived on tea and a cherry Bakewell tart at the A.B.C.—one tart a piece—and the conversation was about what we would do when we became stars. There was never a moment's doubt and never a moan. Jimmy Stewart, who would change his name to 'Stewart Granger', did go on a bit about the difficulty of getting a screen test, but the depression as such didn't get a look-in. We didn't, of course, have television pumping out misery and disruption to us fifteen hours a day. We had the wireless, which was something quite different. It broadcast calm and reassurance ... and late night dance music from all the best hotels in town. Somebody even had a gramophone, we were in clover—vicarious clover, but clover.

The records, as mentioned, cost a couple of bob, or it may have been two and a kick, in the financial parlance then current. Carroll Gibbons was marvellous to dance to, with the reservations concerning tempi mentioned earlier. 'Cuddle and sway to' would be more accurate, perhaps—I, for one, lived in a wooden extension to a house that measured nine by five. The walls bent if you leaned against them which of course you didn't when dancing. He also provided background music when you were studying, for instance, the last scene of *Othello*, though I can't think what I was doing studying the last scene of *Othello*—the casting was baroque to say the least, I was as thin as a rake and only five feet nine. As I worked my way through 'It is the cause, it is the cause, my soul . . .' which is the lead up to the bit where he strangles Desdemona, I had a borrowed record on a borrowed portable, playing Mr Gibbons' version of 'I guess I'll have to change my plan'.

When I left Drama School and went on the stage a mysterious change came over my life. For some reason which, to this day, escapes me, wealthy mothers began to look upon me as deb fodder. I was doing well, and even had my picture in *The Tatler*, but I had nothing in the bank. A good financial catch I wasn't; hungry I was, permanently, so I accepted every invitation that came my way. I owned evening dress—if you were an actor it was obligatory—and was to be seen not infrequently dancing, say, to Roy Fox's band at Monseigneur where Al Bowlly sang the vocals, and at the Café de Paris where Al also sang the vocals, as I recall—he did float around and Lew Stone's band was at the Café for a spell. He even sang them with Carroll.

In the thirties, commercial radio had to reach this country from Europe. It is consistent with the British foible that we might listen to music that advertised jam provided we twiddled the knob on the wireless half an inch to the right. The lunacy shone to the full when you realized the broadcasts were recorded freely in London and flown to Europe to be sent back to us over what we then called 'the ether'. You couldn't imagine anything more British if you tried hard. Carroll fulfilled these stints with a small group he called 'The Boy Friends'. (Innocence continued to hold sway. If it hadn't you can be sure that the British powers-that-were would have disallowed the title.)

'On the air', Carroll's wireless signature (he wrote the melody), announced that Carroll was on the commercial air too. Singing the vocals was a rather special lady named Anne Lenner. She had two sisters, Shirley Lenner and Judy Shirley. Anne Lenner was an interesting choice by Carroll, since she avoided the prevalent temptation to sing in pseudo-American; it was an English voice and, to me, most attractive. Moreover, it fitted perfectly the sound Carroll made, which was far from being an American sound. The American polish it had, yes, but the style was the very best of British.

We in Britain continued to dance and sing into the late thirties, unaware or determined to be unaware of the marching noises made across the water by the *Nazional-Sozialistische-Deutsche-Arbeiter-Partei* which Winston Churchill was soon to refer to with scathing and intentional mispronunciation as 'the Narzees'. In 1939, shortly before the sluice gates opened, Carroll went to America for a holiday, and was caught there when war broke out. I had quite a few American friends who were caught on this side of the Atlantic and I recall the anxious waiting to go back. That an American should be anxious to leave America and travel west to east confounded the United States authorities. It took Carroll some time to convince them he'd rather be here than there. At the Savoy he was welcomed back with open arms and more than one open bottle as the year came to an end.

The Savoy Hotel Grill and Restaurant continued to be an oasis of reassurance in the wartime desert. It was an American, too, who wrote the melody of one of the most British of songs, 'A nightingale sang in Berkeley Square'. His name was Manning Sherwin. The words were by Eric Maschwitz. In the atmosphere of bewilderment that obtained in mid-1940 it was odd to hear this performed in the revue *New Faces*. The song was a piece of musical romance so out of keeping with gas masks, anti-aircraft emplacements and the uniforms that were everywhere to be seen in London that it seemed, as it were, to put us in keeping again with sanity. It was an incongruously romantic lyric for a public that preferred its lunacy linked with lovers. To my mind it inspired more confidence than a dozen Tipperarys. It was always on request and Carroll played it and played it, while Anne Lenner sang the lyric beautifully.

When the ironmongery began to fall and even nightingales were—for the time being, anyway—silenced, the Orpheans continued to be heard. One night there was an interruption. Carroll told me of a near-miss in the Strand that tumbled him from the stool of his white piano and jogged a few musicians off the rostrum. It happened that Noël Coward was in the restaurant. Coward didn't play the piano at all well but he loved doing it, and before Carroll could recover his composure—and his stool—Noël was on it, playing and singing. His opening line, delivered with due Coward emphasis, was 'And a nightingale sang in Berkeley Square!' The diners gave him a sitting ovation for that and Carroll flopped into a nearby chair to join in the applause. Noël continued playing and leading a sing-song. The anti-aircraft guns were going full blast in Hyde Park and could be heard for miles. What with the shells going up and the bombs coming down, it was an interesting concert.

Carroll and I met in the spring of 1943. A song I had written for an Army concert in 1940, my first words and music, called 'I'm going to get lit up when the lights go up in London' had found a home at last in the Sid Field show *Strike a New Note* at

Carroll Gibbons with Anne Lenner – a very special vocalist.

the Prince of Wales' Theatre. Peter Maurice published it and one day, at the invitation of Jimmy Phillips the boss, I called in at Tin Pan Alley. Jimmy was in the office with Joe Brannelley. They said they wanted me to meet the man who would be the first to record the song. This statement was, in itself, enough to cause a temporary paralysis but when Carroll Gibbons walked in and said 'H-hullo' my cup ranneth all over Jimmy Phillips' floor. It was a strange coincidence that Debroy—or Bill—Somers, Carroll's predecessor as conductor of the Orpheans, had made the theatre arrangement and was conducting the pit orchestra nightly at the Prince of Wales'. When Carroll's recording was issued I bought three copies, stacked them on my machine and played them again and again; I couldn't believe my luck. I was lucky too in that the song caught on. Apart from anything else it enabled me to pay more frequent visits to the Savoy restaurant, no longer as deb fodder but under my own steam.

I used to like using the river entrance. For one thing it was the entrance Winston Churchill used, though he didn't come for dancing. As you went up the long staircase and made your winding way to the restaurant you noticed—or at least I did—an unusual smell. Was it ozone? A palmy smell ... well, they were palmy days so why not? It was exhilarating, I remember it vividly. If I close my eyes I may ascend at any time ... On we go, the distant music becoming gradually louder as we make our way ... We drop our coats ... and here we are in the restaurant. We are greeted by and greet Santorelli, the *maître d'hôtel*. Our table is in the corner. We notice that the band is playing rhumba music and Roberto Ingles is at the piano, but Carroll is coming in now to make the changeover. He stands beside Roberto and, without the smallest hiatus in the music, puts his fingers on to the keyboard as the rhumba master lifts his. Roberto lifts the rest of him and suddenly it is Carroll sitting in his place and playing the rhumba music. It continues as the other musicians change places. Now we have the Orpheans playing the last touch of rhumba ... a flourish and the dancers end their dance and applaud ... Now begins the unmistakable and unmatchable sound we came to hear and dance to. We take the floor.

Carroll was a hard worker. He had to be to achieve such apparent ease at the keyboard and for his band to maintain such polish. Once weekly they rehearsed at the Savoy, for the Savoy. There were recordings, radio rehearsals and appearances. Throughout wartime there were the Sunday trips here, there and 'somewhere in England' to entertain the Forces. Moreover, Carroll was a great stayer-up. Often he played cards until the large hours. Usually he was in his office by eleven a.m., choosing music, leafing through orchestrations. I encountered this unsparing professionalism at first hand in the early spring of 1945. Carroll joined Leslie Henson in presenting *Leslie Henson's Gaieties* at the Winter Garden Theatre. They asked me if I had any songs they could include. I always had songs and three of them went into the *Gaieties*. Carroll was to conduct the orchestra in the pit. I remember his strict injunction to his musicians at the first band call. 'No deputies,' he said. 'I don't want any of you putting in deputies. When I look around me at the overture every night I want to see the same faces. O.K.?' I never did understand a musician being prepared to let another step into his place. It seemed to me that it was a belittlement of his own contribution to the orchestra that he should feel anyone else might manage as well. There were no deputies.

The last dress rehearsal for the *Gaieties* went on almost ad nauseam. Poor Leslie Henson, who was directing too, had polished everyone but himself—he had sacrificed his own sketches to the extra rehearsal of other actors. Carroll looked white and really ill as the time drew near for opening. The rehearsal finished, I think, half an hour before the audience arrived. I had invited Robert and Iris Nesbitt to be my guests for the evening. We moved into our seats and sat waiting for the overture. I was apprehensive, knowing what a kerfuffle must be going on backstage and in the band room. The musicians trooped into their places. Suddenly, a pale but beautifully spruce Carroll Gibbons—white-tied and tailed—stepped up on to the pit podium. Half an hour earlier I had seen him in his shirt sleeves and braces, the honest sweat pouring. A roar of applause. He acknowledged it with his head as he turned his back to us, raising his arms to begin the music. From the first beat it was superb, with not the slightest sign of weariness from all the preparation. I wondered, though, whether Carroll would stay up all night again tonight . . .

In the late forties I lived in George Street, W.1, in a block of flats called 'Cumberland Mansions'. I discovered that Carroll was living opposite in the rather grander Bryanston Court. He came, inevitably, to call and played my piano quite a lot. Hutch had played on it too, it was becoming expensive to speak to that piano. I asked him about the trick of playing single notes in the bass. 'Simple,' he said and showed me. For him, it was; I tried and it wasn't simple enough for me.

Carroll was a great party man, and one of his party tricks—he used it in his broadcast programmes—was to make up a tune on the spot. He would ask the assembly to call out three notes. 'A, F sharp, D . . .' they might say. He would play A, F sharp, D a couple of times, feeling his way, then would go off into instant composition. Every year we invited him to be our guest at the Green Room Club dinner. He looked like a happy schoolboy when we asked him to play. Notes would be called out . . . he began his instant composition and lured me into trying instant lyric writing. Some peculiar marriages of words and music were made.

Time ran out far too soon for Carroll. The attachment to work . . . and play. The late nights and all that goes with them. He seemed determined not to miss a moment in enjoyable company—nor a moment being enjoyable company. He wrote a song with Douglas Furber for *Leslie Henson's Gaieties*. The words were Duggie's but Carroll, I'm quite sure, fell in with the idea.

> IT WAS SWELL WHILE IT LASTED . . .
> BUT IT COULDN'T LAST FOR TOO LONG . . .

He died of a heart attack in London on May 10th, 1954. He was fifty-one years old.

I remember another party trick of Carroll's. Not so much a trick as a throwaway song at the piano. It began:

WELL, GOODBYE NOW,
I'LL BE SEEIN' YOU;
GOODBYE NOW,
GLAD TO'VE MET'N UP WITH YOU . . .

Those lines ran fairly true to rhythmic form. Now came a nonsense duel between words and music, the words pouring out while the rhythm continued—you wondered if the words would make it in time. They did—just.

YEAH, I'LL MEET YOU DOWN AT BRIGHTON
NEXT WEDNESDAY NIGHT
WE'LL GO INTO ONE OF THOSE PRIZE BALLROOMS
AND MAYBE IF WE'RE GOOD ENOUGH
THE GUY THAT OWNS THE HALL'LL GIVE US
ONE OF THOSE PRIZE DOLLS AS WELL,
GOODBYE NOW . . .

We were back on the beam . . .

I'LL BE SEEIN' YOU;
GOODBYE NOW,
GLAD TO'VE MET'N UP WITH YOU . . .

Another duel:

NO, I'M AFRAID YOU CAN'T TAKE ME HOME, YOU SEE
MY FATHER'S A NIGHT WATCHMAN, GETS HOME
ABOUT 4.30, 5 IN THE MORNING, HATES TO SEE YOUNG MEN
STREWN ALL OVER THE VERANDAH—

Back for the rhythmic, old-time finish . . .

NO, GOODBYE NOW,
I'LL BE SEEIN' YOU
AND WE'LL BOTH HAVE A REAL GOOD TIME!

It's a mouthful of a song. Carroll recorded it once for a laugh. He made it in one take, he didn't need to do it again. I wish he could, though. All of it.

AL JOLSON
Painting the Clouds

Al in the 1927 part-talkie role which brought him world-wide
recognition.

AL JOLSON

Jolson had a song about a rainbow:

> THERE'S A RAINBOW ROUND MY SHOULDER
> AND A SKY OF BLUE ABOVE . . .

he sang. Not only did he wear a rainbow himself, he had the knack of handing them out in performance so that every member of his audience would leave the theatre richer by a rainbow.

Jolson was born Asa Yoelson. When, is debatable. It is not unknown for people in entertainment to push the year forward a little when forced to recall their birth date (v. Cole Porter). Al remembered it as 1888 but we could be nearer the mark if we made it 1885. To ascertain the absolute truth we would have to travel to Leningrad in Russia where they might not be helpful, especially since the birth certificate, if it exists, would read 'St Petersburg'.

Asa's father, Moses Reuben Yoelson, was a cantor at the local synagogue and hoped that at least one of his boys would follow him. His wife, Naomi, had borne him two—Hirsch and Asa—and two daughters, Rose and Etta. Russia was not yet red but it had Cossacks and, all in all, Moses Reuben thought his family might do better in the New World. The turn of the century saw much trekking from East to West, and quite a number of the fugitives would enrich the American way of entertainment. Despite proudly glowing reports that filtered back to Russia from earlier emigrants, the shrewder dreamers about escape, like

Moses Reuben Yoelson, guessed that life in America would not be so easy. One thing was felt to be certain: there would be no pogroms.

Cantor Yoelson left Naomi in charge and went ahead to pave the way. It took the cautious Cantor four years, it was not until 1894 that the family were reunited, in Washington D.C. The waiting, however, had taken its toll and Naomi Yoelson died one year later, leaving Rose to become 'mother'. Brother Hirsch was thirteen, Asa ten, when they began selling newspapers to help out. They also began to haunt theatres and their father Moses read the riot act, making up his own commandments . . . 'Thou shalt not entertain'. When Hirsch ran away to New York, Asa followed, which didn't please Hirsch since running away is best done solo. Both wound up on the doorstep of a reluctant uncle. They made a brief stay, after which Hirsch was given a couple of bucks and shown the doorstep again and Asa was packed off home. A fortnight later he was back in New York. Al told the story and retold it often . . . probably, like Shakespeare's old soldier from Agincourt, 'with fresh exaggerations every time'.

I can remember the first job I ever got singing. I was passing the stage door of a theatre on 29th Street in New York City. The great Fay Templeton was rehearsing a new song. I stood there and listened . . . and listened until I was singing it along with her. Finally I remembered I was hungry—you get awfully hungry when you're eleven years old . . . so I started walking down towards the Bowery . . . and I kept hearing the piano player playing that tune. I kept getting hungrier too. I didn't have any money so I went into a joint named McGurk's or something like that . . . I asked the guy if he'd give me a cup of coffee if I'd sing a song. He said 'O.K.' The song was 'Rosie, you are my posie'—the one I'd heard Fay Templeton sing . . .

Before achieving the voice we came to know, Al suffered the agonies of the young male whose notes descend from the higher to the lower register. He had sung treble from the gallery when

Eddie Leonard invited the audience to sing. He was such a success at this that Leonard approached his father for permission to include him in the act. The horrified Cantor refused to give it but when the same offer came from Aggie Beeler, Asa ignored his father's repeated objection and set off on the road with Miss Beeler in *The European Sensation*. It was after this that the voice took a break.

Brother Hirsch, meanwhile, was making his own small success. He changed his name to 'Harry' and Asa became 'Al'. They joined forces in an act called 'The Hebrew and the Cadet', and later became singing waiters. They made a trio with Joe Palmer and nipped the 'e' from their second names; the 'Y' became 'J' too, they were billed as 'Jolson, Palmer and Jolson—A Little of Everything'. In Brooklyn, Al was advised to try what the entertainment world calls 'blacking up'. In black face Al was immediately at home: the timbre of the voice fitted, and the white gloves added emphasis to his broad gestures. This was in 1904. Al would continue to appear in this make-up for the next twenty-seven years.

Harry Jolson left the act and made a success in fresh fields. Critics referred to Al as 'Harry Jolson's brother'—but not for long. Al went solo and began to earn big money. He was a big spender too, at the race tracks. He horrified his poor father again by marrying Henrietta Keller, a gentile. She did try to get him to put something by for a rainy day, but for Al there would be no such days. 'I shall be a millionaire,' he told her. 'I'm the world's greatest entertainer . . .'

Al wasn't the only one who thought highly of Al. Lew Dockstader of the famous Dockstader's Minstrels saw him and signed him on the spot. It was now only half a short step to Broadway. The Shuberts bought out Dockstader, lock, stock and Jolson, and in no time Al was appearing at the newly opened Winter Garden Theatre. The year was 1911, Al was twenty-six. His first show for the Shuberts was *La Belle Paree*. One critic wrote: 'Equally amusing is Al Jolson . . .' Equal to whom has been lost in time. 'Whether he is Alfred or Albert this modest seceder from Vaudeville will not divulge ...' 'Modest' was a strange word, as Al had an ego that would float a battleship. Was it reluctance to lay himself open to possible anti-semitism?

In *Vera Violetta* he starred with the delectable Gaby de Lys. (I didn't see her, being too young, but my father, who was something of a judge, found her delectable.) Al persuaded the Shuberts to let him sing in the aisles and, later, to build him a run-out so that he could be among his public. That he achieved this was a particular salute to Al's success, since it entailed the Shuberts' removing a number of seats from the auditorium. He made his first recordings for the Victor Talking Machine Company who labelled him as 'Al Jolson, tenor-comedian'. Show followed show at the Winter Garden: *The Whirl of Society* in 1912, *Honeymoon Express* in 1913, *Dancing Around* in 1914— every one a hit. In 1916, *Robinson Crusoe Jr* included the song 'Where did Robinson Crusoe go with Friday on Saturday night?'

There was around Broadway at the time a young, talented egocentric named George Gershwin. He was aged nineteen or thereabouts, and had written several songs, one of which had found its way into a show and had been swamped by girlie rompings. There's nothing like girlie rompings for swamping a song. It wouldn't be easy to imagine a room capable of holding Gershwin and Jolson, even without their hats, but one did. It contained a piano. Where there was a piano Gershwin would be sitting at it playing the melodies of Gershwin—and Jolson needed no persuasion to sing. I note that I have fallen into the easiest of descriptive traps by speaking of Gershwin 'songs'; they were, of course, half-songs, since Gershwin wrote only the melodies. The one that had been girl-swamped had words by Irving Caesar, who would later join Vincent Youmans in writing *Tea for Two*. Gershwin sat at this particular piano and played this particular Gershwin tune. 'How does the lyric go?' asked Jolson, and Gershwin, who might not have thought the lyric necessary, told him. Jolson sang it there and then and enjoyed the rendering. He put the ditty into his 1918 show *Sinbad* and such are the vagaries of theatre that the flop song was an immediate hit. The kind of hit, moreover, that bade fair to make a standard. The name of the song is 'Swanee'.

Songs and their creation fascinated Jolson. On his first recording for Victor he had sung one written by George M. Cohan. Cohan was an all-rounder—an actor-manager, a composer-lyricist, a playwright, a singer ... It may be that Al was irked by Cohan's versatility. He longed to have his name on a song copy in the writing credits. It is felt in some areas that Jolson's contributions to the songs that bear his name—and there are quite a few—were limited to the publicity he was able to give them in performing them. In 1920 appeared a song called 'Avalon'. 'I found my love in Avalon across the bay ...' Composed, it says on the copy, 'by Vincent Rose ... lyrics by Al Jolson and Buddy de Sylva'. De Sylva was no slouch at lyric writing and shouldn't have needed help, unless it was from Lew Brown, when putting words to Ray Henderson's music. The melody of Avalon rang a bell for one Giacomo Puccini, who was still alive at the time. Hadn't he, he asked himself, run off those same notes when he created the tenor aria from *Tosca*? He sued the writers of *Avalon* and won. They had to pay a fair share of their royalties to the man who had preceded them, operatically. Whether only Rose was affected, since the lyrics were quite different from those in *Tosca*, is not recorded.

Al had been a success on Broadway for twelve years when a building opened bearing his name. The Jolson Theatre stood on 59th Street. The first show at the new house was *Bombo*—I suspect the word 'bomb' in connection with the American theatre had not yet acquired its meaning of 'flop'. In *Bombo* Al introduced 'April Showers'. The eponymous star at the Jolson Theatre was thirty-six years old ... or thirty-five or thirty-four; or, according to Jolson, thirty-three. Whatever his age, it was an achievement. Al had taken Broadway and the Great White Way had taken Al. 'Just keep on looking for a bluebird', he sang to them. Bluebirds were not too easy to spot in the years following the First World War, unless you were up there in the clouds yourself, with the politicians. But if Al told you to look ... you felt sure there was a sporting chance there might be one.

At that time, if you wanted to hear Al Jolson sing you had to be where he was or own what the Victor Talking Machine Company would call a Victrola and a few disc records. The records made in those early, pre-electric days tended to make a singer sound as though he was singing at one end of a tunnel to you listening at the other. Al's were better than most because of the quality of his voice, and they sold well. But, with no wireless, no television, no talking pictures, he was cut off from the world he wanted to embrace. He took to touring. *Bombo* toured extensively but the nearer he came to his public, the farther away his marriage faded. His big love, the theatre, dwarfed domesticity; he was divorced in 1922 and promptly married Ethel Delmar who was in the cast of *George White's Scandals*.

Al continued to work at a tremendous pitch. Since 1913, in company with colleagues like Eddie Cantor, George Jessel, the Astaires, and the Marx Brothers, he had appeared consistently on Sunday nights at the Winter Garden Theatre. Seven nights a week meant nothing to Al—and meant everything. He did display a ruthlessness that was not always to be admired. In 1923 the great cinema visionary, D. W. Griffith, cast him in a silent picture with the prophetic title, *Mammy's Boy*. Al didn't like the rushes and walked out of the film. Standing to lose $100,000 Griffith sued, but had to settle for $3,000. The basis of Jolson's case was that he had signed no contract. In the theatre we tend to feel that a promise is a promise, whether spoken or written. In the early cinema, especially when dealing with an august figure like Griffith, I would have thought the same principle applied.

In 1925, Al starred as a negro jockey in *Big Boy*. It was presented at the Winter Garden because the Jolson Theatre already had a success called *The Desert Song*. The *New York Times* acclaimed him: 'Even more vibrant than ever . . . A great man of the theatre is Mr Jolson.' In *Big Boy* he introduced a song with another prophetic title, 'California, here I come!'

In the same year, 1925, talking pictures began to creep into the cinemas. Dr Lee de Forest was the inventor, and I remember vividly the excitement of seeing and hearing my first 'De Forrest Phonofilm'. After a silent programme we heard a voice from nowhere saying 'Ladies and gentlemen, there is no gramophone in any way connected with this picture.' There wasn't. It was sound-on-film. The subjects were short novelty items presenting people like Raymond Newell, the baritone, who was then a concert singer but would go into musical theatre, Dick Henderson, the Yorkshire comedian (father of Dickie Henderson), and another very popular comedian of the day, Billy Merson. I didn't know then that, in America, they were making these Phonofilms with American artists. Dr Lee de Forrest had sold his invention to Warner Brothers who made a short called *April Showers* in which Al sang three songs. The sound-on-film system had its problems—something to do with amplification, they said, though it may have had something more to do with expense. The fact was that, in 1927, when Warner Brothers decided to make *The Jazz Singer* they used sound recorded on huge discs which the film operator had to play on a turntable in the cinema operating box. They called it 'Vitaphone'.

The subject Warner Brothers chose for the first talking feature—which, in the event, was to be half a talking feature—was a Broadway stage hit that starred George Jessel. They invited Jessel to play in the film but there was a disagreement over terms. The picture, or that part of it that would not be the silent mixture-as-before, was to be not exactly a talkie, since only the songs would be synchronized—if you don't take that word too literally. Jessel put too high a price on his services, they decided. They went to Eddie Cantor, who turned the offer down, perhaps because Jessel had made such a success in the part on Broadway. Al, of course, was undisturbed by any such thoughts. He accepted a share in the profits and collected nearly twenty times the sum they had refused to pay Jessel.

In *The Jazz Singer* Al's ego carried the day. Instead of merely singing his first song he had a few words with the audience in the scene, using the catchphrase he would make famous: 'You ain't heard nothin' yet.' To cinema audiences, used to the silent

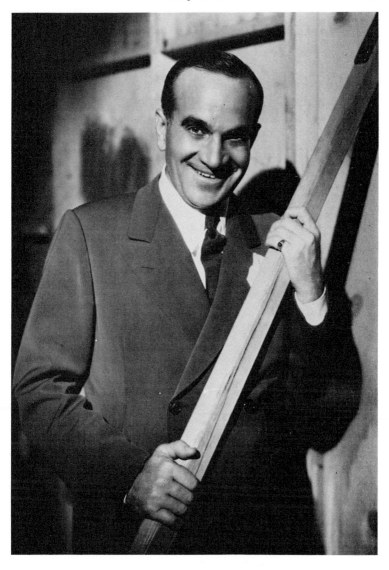

Al – 'the world's greatest entertainer'.

grimaces of the Johns, Barrymore and Gilbert, the result was electrifying. Or Vitaphonic. Jolson's ad-libbing in the scene with his mother floored poor Eugenie Besserer, who wasn't really up to making answer. Al didn't need her to answer in any case, he would have been quite happy to play the scene with himself. The astonishing result is that the acting had the style and the reality of a much later date. *The Jazz Singer* opened in October 1927 and was a world wide sensation. Its success pulled Warner Brothers out of the red just as, six years later when they had sunk again, *42nd Street*, starring the third Mrs Al Jolson, would perform the same rescue operation.

Al and his second wife had parted company in 1926. The co-respondent was, again, the theatre or, more accurately, entertainment in general. But Al would still not admit to having room in his life only for this one love. In New York to promote *The Jazz Singer*, he met and married Ruby Keeler and proceeded to promote her career. His follow-up talkie, *The Singing Fool*, was an even greater success than *The Jazz Singer*. The takings were a record that would remain unbroken for ten years until honourably shattered by *Gone With the Wind*. Al now embraced radio and went full ahead into recording.

Hollywood, flushed almost to black face with two successes, proceeded to cast Jolson in picture after picture with the same pathos—and bathos. All had very nearly the same story. *Sonny Boy* in which little Davy Lee died, *Say it with Songs*, in which he came to life again in order to be run over ... *Mammy*, in 1930, clinched the matter. The public, by this time a public many millions strong, was tiring of Al Jolson. After making the film version of *Big Boy*, a modest success only on celluloid, he returned to Broadway to star in *Wonder Bar* wearing white face for the first time. This was merely another modest success—perhaps they didn't know who he was. Modesty didn't go with the Jolson image—it was smash hit or nothing. He made *Hallelujah, I'm a Bum!* for United Artists in '33. (The title was bowdlerized for Britain where 'bum' meant something else; 'Tramp' was substituted.) It was a charming movie with a score by Rodgers and Hart, but it was several cuts above the general public with its rhymed dialogue spoken to music. Jolson found himself in the doldrums.

He could still earn enormous sums in Vaudeville, as much as $17,500 a week. But the ego doesn't live by dollars alone. His promotion of Ruby Keeler meant that her career had the wind behind it, but her success was no help domestically. He made the film of *Wonder Bar* in 1934 and in the following year co-starred with Ruby Keeler in *Go Into Your Dance*. Neither movie was the success he had hoped it would be.

Jolson's star was growing dimmer, it seemed. He could earn money with no difficulty, but acclaim eluded him. It was like pressure on a main artery. He should have been but never, I think, could have been a family man. Ruby Keeler and he had adopted a son in 1935 but in 1939 the two were divorced. In the same year he played in the movie *Rose of Washington Square*, taking third billing after Alice Faye and Tyrone Power. This was Hollywood's assessment of the star who, twelve years earlier, had set the motion picture world on its ear. There was no doubt who claimed first attention in the picture. The songs may have been familiar but when Al gave us 'Toot-toot-tootsie, goodbye' that old black face magic was there. The 'world's greatest entertainer'—Al had said it but the world had roared unanimous agreement—was still aglow.

Goodbyes were going to be the order the world over. The Second World War was on our doorstep in Britain, and many people in entertainment were to suffer an interval in their careers, which they would find it hard to make up for in Act Two. Many an up-and-comer looked like being a goner. In November 1940, a year before America entered the war, Al played his last stage show on Broadway, but only after putting up $100,000 of his own money to back it. It closed after 150 performances. Jolson, in common with dozens of his star colleagues, went overseas to entertain the Forces. By the oddest stroke of fortune, it re-made him. He was in his mid-fifties and singing to a new generation who were loving it. He was, too, but he picked up a malaria germ in West Africa and had to return to America. Against medical advice he continued to entertain on home base, and it was while engaged in this that he met and fell in love with a hospital technician named Erle Galbraith. He underwent an operation in which part of a lung had to be removed but rallied in time, not only to marry Miss Galbraith but also to appear as himself in the Gershwin film life story, *Rhapsody in Blue*.

After the war the Mayor of New York issued an invitation. The home-spun philosopher, Will Rogers, said once, 'On Broadway they never give you a dinner until you can't afford to buy one.' In the case of Al Jolson this didn't apply but the remark has a relevant flavour. The Mayor of the day was Jimmy Walker. Handing a scroll to Jolson, he said:

'It is an honour for the American Veterans' Committee, on behalf of the men and women in the Armed Forces who won our fight for freedom, to salute their outstanding friend, Mr Al Jolson. During the days of pain, loneliness and boredom, this great entertainer cheered millions of us who were scattered over the earth. Every theatre of war knew him and was brightened by his presence.'

In 1945 Warner Brothers, whose bacon—if his father would overlook the phrase—Al had saved seventeen years earlier, were approached about filming his life story. They turned the project down. The head of Columbia Pictures saw and heard Al at a Hollywood concert and decided to take a chance on the movie. Jolson was desolate at not being allowed to play himself, though he did pre-record all the songs. Larry Parks was excellent visually as Jolson but who could have imitated the inimitable, the Jolson voice? The film The Jolson Story was a huge hit, Al, for his percentage alone, collecting $5,000,000. But, more than this, Al was a star again. His records sold by the million and he was, once again, sitting on top of the entertainment world. He was in demand as guest on the top radio programmes, then was given his own series and became host instead of guest. There was the inevitable sequel to *The Jolson Story*—Hollywood never could rest on a laurel. The title was *Jolson Sings Again*. Larry Parks starred, Al sang the songs and this time made a brief appearance. The reception was well up to expectation. Jolie—his name to his colleagues—was riding high. Young Erle Galbraith, who had married a professionally forgotten man, discovered that she was the wife of what, today, we might call a 'superstar', though I've never been quite sure about these terms. They are part of the currency debasement, I suppose. 'Super' did, I'm afraid, become 'mega' but when it, in turn, suffers devaluation . . . what then?

The Korean war was on and Al decided he should be on his entertaining travels again. He expressed publicly his views about this area of work:

> 'It's only today that I'm really playing what they call "the big time". Of all the wonderful audiences I've played to in my whole life, the ones that have given me the greatest thrill were thousands of miles away from Broadway . . .'

Behind his feelings, too, there was perhaps a need to prove to himself and to all whom it might concern that Jolie, at sixty-four, was as young as when he'd first shouldered that rainbow. His doctor said 'No', his young wife said 'Please don't', and even his accompanist, Harry Akst—composer of 'Baby face'—was reluctant. Harry had been with him during the earlier war and knew the stresses that lay ahead.

Playing again 'the big time', Al gave it everything he had—literally. After two gruelling weeks he and Harry flew to Los Angeles. The most immediate commitment would be a guest appearance on the Bing Crosby Show to be recorded in San Francisco. He left on October 23rd, 1950, Harry Akst travelling with him. At the airport he said goodbye for the last time to young Mrs Jolson. He never made the Crosby show. He died in his San Francisco hotel room after a heart attack. The lights were lowered on Broadway in his honour but a greater light had gone out than would ever shine there again.

For nearly half a century Al Jolson had carried his talent, in person or through the medium of the talking picture he had helped to launch, to the farthest cities, towns and villages of the world. From these same outposts the tributes now came flooding. 'The world's greatest entertainer' was a common phrase. Charlie Chaplin described Al as 'a great instinctive artist who personified the poetry of Broadway, its vitality, its vulgarity . . . its aims, its dreams . . .'

Chaplin added that only a shadow of the real Al Jolson appeared in films. It may be so. But the Jolson shadow, on screen and Victrola, had substance enough to give a lifetime of memories to two, even three generations . . . with more to come.

IVOR NOVELLO
Crest of the Wave

The right profile of Ivor Novello as displayed in the silent film *The White Rose*.

IVOR NOVELLO

Some thought that David Ivor Davies, despite the Welshness of the name, had a touch of Italian. This may have stemmed from the fact that his grandfather, Jacob Davies, admired the Italian contralto Clara Novello and named his daughter after her. Young David dropped the 'David' and the 'Davies' and became Ivor Novello. Clara Novello Davies (Ivor called her 'ma'am' and was not discouraged from so doing) was a teacher of singing with a reputation and, it seems, a presence that spilled over the principality into the national and international scene. She was a child prodigy who taught the piano at seven years old, and at twelve formed a Ladies' Choir. She went on forming choirs until she died at the age of eighty-two.

Ivor was born in Cardiff on January 15th, 1893. His mother had been teaching only two hours earlier, I don't think her astonished pupil even knew she was expecting anyone else. To ladies—and others—who later swooned at Novello's facial beauty it may come as a surprise that his parents didn't think much of his looks early on. Babies are not noted for immediate good looks but Ivor had a huge nose to boot, and was considered downright ugly.

His father, David Davies, was, according to one description, 'a darling old peasant'. He worked—when he worked—for the Cardiff Council but being a Welshman was musical too. The name of the family house, unpronounceable by the non-Welsh, being translated meant 'grove of nightingales'. Ivor remembered it in these words:

'When I was a child my mother was the centre of musical life in Cardiff and our house in Cathedral Road was always full of musicians, singers and actors. Practically every visiting celebrity stayed with us and I suppose that this proximity to the great and near-great gave me a taste for glamour which I have never lost.'

Before Ivor Novello achieved this glamour—not his own, which I think he may have been born with, but the glamour which he purveyed for our delight—there were many vicissitudes, domestic and professional. For me Ivor was four distinct people. Firstly he was the silent film star I watched as a tot in the Rink Cinema at Sydenham in South London ... well, not quite a tot, since I was in the back row holding hands with a girl from the grammar school. *The Rat* was the title of the picture. Novello was a household name. I heard it bruited in my household that he had written one of the great songs of the First World War. That made two people. On my theatre visits to the West End, both while I was at school and later as a drama student, I saw Novello appearing on the stage in his own slight little comedies. Highly successful some were, but I think the greater part of his audience had come to see the beautiful film star in person—Novello number three. Number four was the grand-scale writer of shows that filled—in all senses—Drury Lane Theatre in the thirties, shows with music that brought for me, the Novello story full of circle.

Ivor sang soprano when young. He even stepped in for an absent lady when his mother was conducting her choir—which couldn't have done him a lot of good. The voice did, though. It gained him a scholarship at Magdalen College Choir School, Oxford where at fifteen he was already writing music. The voice stayed with him until he was rising seventeen. He was devastated when it broke. My feeling is that the lateness of the development might have been responsible for the fact that he had no singing voice as an older man when he could well have used one.

He had studied under Dr Brewer, the organist at Gloucester Cathedral. Brewer thought him the laziest pupil he'd ever had. 'I like to write spontaneously,' Ivor said later to Noël Coward. It's as good an excuse as any. Interestingly, Noël who had a very limited knowledge of music, worked hard at it with Elsie April whereas Ivor who did know tended, according to the expert Alec Robertson, to be slipshod:

> He had a tremendous theatrical instinct and he knew that people were looking forward to a lovely tune. The preparation for that tune, the introduction, was sometimes merely—in the old theatrical phrase—'until ready'. That wasn't good enough to me, at all. Then came the verse. He didn't spend much trouble on the verse because the refrain was coming after. In other words, he was not a wholehearted craftsman. One of the very best things he did is 'Love is my reason for living' from *Perchance to Dream*. Here you get, in the introduction, his feeling for Debussy-like harmonies and you get that again in the verse—with quite remarkable modulations...

About his own reason for living Ivor was undecided. His parents couldn't afford to send him to university but his 'ma'am' wouldn't hear of his following his father's guidance and entering a shipping office as a clerk. 'Over my dead body,' she said and father retired from the bout. In 1910—at the age of seventeen— Ivor had his first music published, 'Spring of the year'. At the same time he thought of becoming an actor. He attended an audition for *The Count of Luxemburg* and was engaged. His mother put paid to it by the simple expedient of opening his letters and withholding the ones that gave details about rehearsals. By the time he found out he had lost the job. Some lads would have cut up rough and left home but Ivor's ma'am got away with it.

At eighteen Ivor travelled to America—just for expenses—to write music for a pageant that was never produced. But he was befriended by a singer from the Metropolitan and went night after night to the opera. He met Caruso, he met Melba ... and returned to England fired with new enthusiasms.

He had written quite a few songs by now-and was having some small success with them. 'In the shadows' (not to be confused with the piece Herman Finck composed on a London omnibus), 'In the clouds', 'Up there, blue eyes', 'Why hurry, little river?' ... the titles tell something of the times ... 'Not really', 'in the valley' ... Sometimes he wrote the words too but mostly he collaborated. His mother's pupils were drilled into singing a dozen of his songs at the Aeolian Hall in London. Then came wartime. Ivor told how he came to write the greatest of his melodies:

'Early in the autumn of 1914 Ma'am was urging me to write a popular patriotic song but I was adamant. There had been too many already. "Very well then," she said. "if you don't I will." And she did. If I remember rightly the effort was called "Keep the flag a-flying". To put it mildly, it wasn't very good and might have resulted in the flag being hauled down for all time. She professed to be highly delighted with it and proposed to publish it. So ... to stop any of that nonsense I sat down and wrote a song of my own—that song was "Keep the home fires burning". '

Ivor added:

'I often wonder if she really liked her own song or whether it was a deliberate ruse ...'

The title was Ivor's own idea—no doubt a considered improvement on his mother's. He got a friend of ma'am's, Lena Guilbert Ford, to write the rest of the lyric but, in fact, the title line and the melody make the song.

Ivor Novello was twenty-one, and his music was being hummed and whistled throughout the wartime land and overseas. When the Americans joined the war in 1917 they would whistle it too. George Grossmith invited Ivor to write part of the score for *Theodore and Co.* which opened at the Gaiety Theatre in 1916. In the meantime he had joined the Royal Naval Air Service. His flying instructor was the great—and extremely virile—writer-to-be of the Aldwych farces, Ben Travers. Ben had just suffered a crash, and enjoyed telling the story:

'I walloped into the Firth of Forth at high speed in a torpedo dropper. I survived principally, I think, because I knew so very little of what I was doing.'

Here, the ineffable Ben delivered a superb farce line if ever I heard one:

'On the strength of that crash I was made an instructor.'

He waxed talkative about his new pupil:

'I told Ivor Novello that I ought to participate in any royalties he earned all through his career because if it hadn't been for me I don't think he would have survived the war. He was a most charming and delightful chap to meet but he was the worst possible fellow to learn to fly—he kept composing and singing all the time in the air instead of attending to business. After two or three attempts I said: "You'd better stay on the ground. I'm going to report that you are unfit for flying."'

In 1913 Ivor's mother had rented a flat at No. 11, Aldwych. It sits above the Strand Theatre and, in those days, looked across the street at the Gaiety. Ivor would continue to occupy this flat for the rest of his life. For now, he could contemplate the theatre where *Theodore and Co.* was drawing the town and would run for more than five hundred performances. He spent his war at No. 11, Aldwych and at the Air Ministry. Thus centrally placed, he was able to compose the music for three more successes, *See Saw* at the Comedy, *Arlette* at the Shaftesbury—the theatre the

Germans would bomb out of existence one war later—and *Tabs* starring Bea Lillie at the Vaudeville. He even composed additional songs for Fraser Simpson's *The Southern Maid*. The wartime theatres were flourishing. All over London there was an atmosphere of make-the-most-of-it gaiety. For returning servicemen the contrast with the ghastly goings-on in France must have been dazzling.

As the curtain falls at the end of every war the usual new era begins. It is, alas, never a better era. It is perhaps one of the kindnesses of human experience that we don't know this: we have to learn always—yet again—that we haven't learnt a thing. Ivor, whose one wartime hit was bringing in several thousands of pounds a year, left on a holiday trip to America, taking with him his mother and his special friend, Bobby Andrews. After a five-month stay, during which he was fired again with the enthusiasm only New York can generate, he sailed for England determined to conquer it in some form. He didn't know just which. Somehow music alone wasn't quite enough. Half way across the Atlantic he received a cable asking him to appear in a film. Apparently the director wanted someone with something of a name—not necessarily a name that had anything to do with performing—and who could look as though he had Sicilian forebears. He had seen Ivor's picture in the office of the Daniel Mayer Company—who were my agents when I was young and who presented *Peter Pan* every year, the one fact having nothing to do with the other. 'He's a composer,' they protested, but only mildly since ten per cent is ten per cent. 'Never mind,' said the director, 'we'll soon knock that out of him.'

Ivor was engaged for the film, *The Call of the Blood*, and set off for location in Taormina. The film was successful, so was Ivor. The composer of the music for *Keep the Home Fires Burning* was now a film star, never having set foot on the boards. During the filming he wrote the score for *Who's Hooper?* which ran for 350 performances at the Adelphi. He made two more films, *Miarka* and *Carnival*, then he scored *The Golden Moth* for the stage. Films, music ... music, films ... A to Z was to run at the Prince

of Wales' for 450 performances. It contained a point song—that
is a song whose lyrics are more important than the melody. Dion
Titheradge wrote the words but Ivor set them to memorable
music. This song—'And her mother came too'—was to be one of
Jack Buchanan's biggest successes.

In 1922 Ivor wrote a tune to words by Ben Travers for Ben's
play *Dusky Nipper* at the Criterion. But he still had this mother-
defeated longing to appear on a stage. He achieved this at last at
the age of twenty-nine—pretty late, really, for an actor—playing
a five minute scene in *Deburau* at the Ambassador's Theatre. He
played a Chinaman named Wu Hoo Git in *The Yellow Jacket* at
the Kingsway and, at the same theatre, a young Spaniard in
Spanish Lovers. The press noticed him in this and actually spoke
well of him—normally they go a bit cold if they think you
shouldn't be doing it. He took the play on tour under his own
management, another new departure, and didn't lose money.
Ivor had made it—to the first rung, anyway—as an actor. It may
be significant that Madame Clara was now living in America
where she was teaching all and sundry and no doubt bossing the
odd one or two. Ivor said once: 'Ma'am ruined more voices than
any other teacher in the business.'

He himself continued, going from success to success, in
movies. He made *The White Rose* in America under the legendary
D. W. Griffith. He saw *Kiki* on the New York stage and appeared
in it with Gladys Cooper at the Playhouse Theatre in London
under the title *Enter Kiki*. The Playhouse, a particularly attractive theatre, in my view, and very comfortable to sit in—you
didn't have to rise to allow people to pass along the row—stands
derelict at the bottom of Northumberland Avenue. *Enter Kiki*
became Exit Kiki in no time at all, the critics coming down like a
pack of Assyrian wolves both on the production and on Ivor.
'Amateurish', they called him—the worst thing a professional can
say about a professional.

Constance Collier advised Ivor to take another play under his
own management into the provinces. His film name would bring
the public in and—I don't think she mentioned this in so many

words—Ivor might learn something about his new trade. He had been trying to promote a film story he had written called *The Rat*. Why not make a play of it, Constance asked. He had never tried writing a play but . . . with her help? Together they wrote and rewrote *The Rat* until it sat up and begged for mercy. It opened in Brighton and to everyone's amazement was a smash hit—with Novello starring. Noël Coward implored him not to bring it into London. Brighton was only the provinces after all and another flop on the scale of *Kiki* could be ruinous. Ivor ignored the advice. He presented and starred in *The Rat* at the Prince of Wales' Theatre, opening in June 1924. It was—and continued to be—a spectacular success. Noël apologized. Ivor said no apology was needed; he was all too grateful to Miss Collier for starting him on this new road.

Novello and Coward were always at pains to deny that rivalry existed between them. Noël beat Ivor to the male lead in the stage version of *The Constant Nymph* in 1926. It was Ivor though who played Lewis Dodd on the screen. He appeared in Noël's *Sirocco* at Daly's in 1927. This was nice of him since, during preliminary talks, Noël had telephoned to say 'Forget it, I'm playing the part', then, an hour later, had telephoned again to say 'The director won't have me, you play it'. *Sirocco* had a memorably terrifying first night with Noël making a curtain speech despite the booing and turning his bottom to the audience as a final silent comment. Ivor made up for the debacle by writing and appearing in *The Truth Game*, a smash hit at the Globe, in the following year.

There were parallels and there were differences. Noël Coward was a personality who gave bravura performances in parts he wrote for himself but was no great actor. Ivor was a better musician than actor but he had bravura too, inherited from his Ma'am. Both enjoyed casting themselves as noblemen—Noël not flying higher than count, Ivor taking the throne in his stride. Both liked playing Frenchmen and had shocking, unrecognizable accents when they did. Friendship, yes. Emulation, perhaps. Rivalry? Yes and no . . .

In 1925 Ivor filmed *The Rat*, and it was at this point that I began seeing him from the back row of the Rink Cinema. He then filmed *The Lodger* and *Downhill*, both directed by Hitchcock. In *Downhill* he played a stalwart public school lad—a bit too stalwart, because when his friend puts a shop girl in Dutch, he takes the blame and is expelled. The film contained the immortal subtitle: 'Does this mean, sir, that I can't play for the Old Boys?' From now on, like me at the Rink, Ivor's music took a back seat. He went to Hollywood but didn't light any fires as an actor—Hollywood was more impressed by the manly Clark Gable type. They had no room for 'the British Adonis', as the American press called him.

My third Novello, the playwright/actor-on-the-stage, made his entrance into my ken. I saw him at the Shaftesbury as a White Russian prince in *I Lived With You* and in *Flies in the Sun* at the Playhouse. In this he cast himself as a silent film star whose career is ruined by the arrival of the talkies. In 1930, in *Symphony in Two Flats*, Ivor himself had made the transition with no difficulty. In *Flies in the Sun* the star commits suicide. I was enormously impressed by the fact that Ivor didn't take a curtain call. As a drama student I already knew that in the theatre there was a tradition that, if you died during the action of a play, you didn't come on at the end to take applause. But ... Ivor Novello? Author and star, the matinée idol to launch a million tea trays? It did occur to this drama student to wonder about *Hamlet*, where nearly everybody is dead at the end...

Party at the Strand Theatre and *Fresh Fields* at the Criterion, both starring Lillian Braithwaite were huge successes. Novello, who had appeared in neither, made it up to himself by playing two parts in *Proscenium*—father and son. The father he based on his own father who had died two years earlier.

It was in the middle thirties that my fourth Novello entered. Music had been cropping up more and more in his plays. In *Murder in Mayfair*, while attempting to play a Frenchman, he accompanied Fay Compton at the piano. One day during the run, Harry Tennent was complaining to Ivor that his Drury Lane Theatre seemed only to have success with pantomime. Spon-

Ivor in the film *The Return of the Rat* – with Mabel Poulton and
Gordon Harker.

taneously—the way he liked to work, we recall—Ivor offered to write a musical play for 'the Lane'. Had he anything in mind, asked Tennent. Then and there Ivor outlined the complete plot of *Glamorous Night*, making it up as he went along—not a very difficult feat, when you consider the plot. Tennent agreed to Novello's request for a forty-piece orchestra, a cast of 120 (this was 1935) and complete *carte blanche* control.

Glamorous Night starred the beautiful and stunningly talented American, Mary Ellis. Mary, who had been a member of the Metropolitan Opera Company, had come to London in 1932 to play in Eugene O'Neill's drama *Strange Interlude*, and had stayed to star in Cochran's *Music in the Air*. It was during the run of this that Ivor had met her. *Glamorous Night* was the first of Ivor's famous Drury Lane hat trick of the thirties. Tennent showed his gratitude by closing the show prematurely to put on panto-mime—the kind of thing managers will do—but Novello was undaunted. The second of the three starred another American, Dorothy Dickson. Acting on Noël Coward's advice (Coward had been there before with his *Cavalcade*), Ivor had given full reign to William Abingdon, the Lane's stage director. The first act of *Glamorous Night* closed with an ocean liner sinking. Now, with *Careless Rapture*, Ivor had an even more impressive effect up his sleeve. It was to put a new phrase into the family language of Dorothy Dickson:

'Ivor said, "Be here at ten o'clock on Thursday morning, they're delivering the earthquake." We all turned up and there it was, it all fell down like a pack of cards, a wonderful thing. I had a line to say ... We were in China, I think ...'

(I didn't bat an eyelid at the uncertainty)...

'... and I had this line just before this earthquake ... I had to say, "My maid says it's earthquake weather." Well, of course it stayed with us. Whenever anything went wrong we'd say, "My maid says its earthquake weather!"'

In any Ivor Novello cast you would find a preponderance of homosexuals—acting, non-acting and those who couldn't quite make up their minds. On the odd occasion when you came across a real male stalwart he would stick out a mile, so to speak. One of these was a friend of mine named Ivan Samson who played a straight part in *Careless Rapture*. I was still a scrawny juvenile scratching around for work when I visited him backstage at his invitation. A matinée performance was in progress and Ivan took me into the wings. I could make out a dimly-lit temple scene with two dancers going at it upstage—and when you say 'upstage' at the Lane it's more like half a mile. 'That's supposed to be Ivor,' said Ivan. 'Isn't it?' I asked. 'No, no,' he said. 'Ivor sends his understudy on at matinées for this bit,' adding with schoolboy glee, 'All those old ladies out there thinking doesn't he dance beautifully!' Then he said, 'The earthquake happens in a minute . . . Tons of muck all over the place. I'm the only one not in the scene.' Another schoolboy chuckle—I never knew anyone to enjoy life as Ivan Samson did. 'It gets everywhere,' he said. 'Up their noses, in their ears, in their hair . . .' At this point a heavily made up crowd chap passed us to make a flouncing entrance '. . . up their skirts . . .' Ivan added. 'They have to have baths and God knows what not, I don't have anything to do with it. I'm in my dressing room having tea. Fancy a cup?'

The third in the hat trick was *Crest of the Wave*. It contained the mixture as before plus, this time, a train crash. One song, a patriotic piece, took us back to 'Keep the home fires burning'— the only difference being that there wasn't a war. (There was a honey of a one coming up but the British ostrich didn't know about that.) 'Rose of England' wasn't in the same class, though.

It isn't easy to guess what Novello had in mind when he chose as his next acting vehicle—and at the same theatre—Shakespeare's *King Henry V*. The up and down of a conductor's baton is one thing, the iambic pentameter quite another. Novello worked as he had never worked before but could not arrive at the virile, warlike character of Shakespeare's play. W. A. Darlington in the

Daily Telegraph wrote: 'He takes the stage well, compensating by his bearing for his lack of inches ... He speaks very clearly, commanding the vast auditorium with ease ...' Obviously, Darlington was doing his best to praise.

Ivor's *Henry* opened at the Lane in September 1938—when other matters, admittedly, were on our minds. For whatever reason, the production closed after three weeks. His next, show was to run, almost continuously, in London and in the provinces for nearly a decade. *The Dancing Years* began at the Lane. Soon after the outbreak of the Second World War, when all theatres were closed by law, the run had to be suspended but Ivor took the production on tour and it played to packed houses for eighteen months. Then it came back to the Adelphi in London to run for a further two years and three months. The neat German invention we called the 'doodle-bug' caused its closure, but the provincial theatres still clamoured.

Madame Novello Davies had died in February of 1943 in the knowledge that her Ivor was for the second time the idol of wartime London. There was a difference in that this war was on our doorstep. A British film called *San Demetrio, London* told the story of a tanker, the *San Demetrio*, trying to carry a cargo of fuel to London and running the gauntlet of German attackers. This, we were reminded, is what some lads were going through to bring us petrol, this is why it was severely rationed. Ivor was suddenly in the headlines for misuse of petrol coupons. An adoring lady fan provided them but the matter was brought to the attention of the police. The Courts may have seen in this an opportunity to bring home to the public the seriousness of black marketry which many insisted upon treating as a game. Ivor's defence was that he needed the petrol to take him to Redroofs, his house near Maidenhead. He was sent to jail for a month. In fact, there was no great hardship—he spent the time in the prison library. On his return to the theatre he received an ovation, and I have no doubt that the message the Courts intended to get across was a missile that failed to explode.

Many and varied were the views on the Novello case. It was

thought by some to be a storm in a petrol can—which could, I suppose, be quite a storm. Others set against those coupons the gifts Ivor was able to offer us with our war-shabby clothes, our tired dreams. 'I can give you the starlight,' said the words to one melody of his. Our skies were empty of stars, empty of everything but German hardware. On the other hand the crew of the *San Demetrio* might have thought the song a poor exchange.

Arc de Triomphe, Ivor's next production, at the Phoenix, failed to attract. The German flying bomb which closed the long-running *The Dancing Years* nipped this one in the bud.

Since *Glamorous Night* Ivor's lyrics had been written by Christopher Hassall who was a poet. I saw him—as an undergraduate—playing Romeo when an O.U.D.S. production directed by John Gielgud was presented for one Sunday night performance at the New Theatre. When I played the part later at drama school I discovered I had inherited his costume. He didn't pursue acting beyond a small part in *Murder in Mayfair*, and I'm not sure how far he went with poetry. As Novello's lyric writer he did very well indeed.

Perchance to Dream opened in April 1945, saw Victory-in-Europe and Victory-in-Japan days and continued to run until the end of 1947. The score contained a number which—had it been launched a year or two earlier—could, I think, have become the song of the Second World War. Alec Robertson remembered how it came to be written:

'Alfred Lunt in America said to Ivor: "I always think of those lilac trees down at Redroofs . . ." Ivor mulled this over and said to Alfred one day, "I've made up a tune about it." This was the tune of 'We'll gather lilacs'. But it was only later that he got Christopher Hassall to write the words to it.'

According to others, Novello wrote both music and lyrics for *Perchance to Dream*. Certainly the lyrics to 'We'll gather lilacs' are more than a touch better than those of the lady who wrote the words for 'Keep the home fires burning'. I am still puzzled though by the plurality of 'lilacs'—I'd have thought it should be 'lilac', but then I'm no horticulturist.

Ivor worked hard—if spontaneously—but new how to play. After the run of *Perchance to Dream* he made a trip to New York for excitement, then gave himself a five-week holiday in Jamaica for relaxation—and for buying a house, emulating Noël Coward who had chosen the same island. He took his entire company to South Africa for short seasons in Johannesburg and Cape Town, then made another trip to Jamaica for a stay in his new house. The ten-month British tour of *Perchance to Dream* was strenuous enough, but Ivor followed that with another New York visit and then several weeks at his house at Montego Bay. This ability to unwind is vitally important to creative folk. If they have it, they usually stay healthy. Tragically, Novello was to be the exception.

His last romantic musical *King's Rhapsody* opened at the Palace Theatre, London, in September 1949. Ivor played the Prince of Murania. Murania, Ruritania ... Drury Lania, what matter where? It was great stuff. This prince, of course, falls in love but has to go back as King to marry another. It was *The Student Prince* and a few more all over again. But Romberg's lad, if you recall, renounces his love. In Ivor's story the conclusion was more to the human point. He marries the chosen lady, produces an heir ... then leaves the baby holding the baby and goes back to his true love. Why, we wondered, dipping into recent actual memory, didn't all Prince-into-King stories have such an ending ...?

During the run of *King's Rhapsody* Ivor had written the book and music for *Gay's the Word*, which would star Cicely Court-neidge. He left the cast at Christmas in 1950 for a prolonged holiday, returning at last in February 1951. He was suntanned but feeling not well. His doctor advised him not to attend the first night of *Gay's the Word* but he went, sitting in a box for all to see. He attended a party afterwards.

He rejoined the cast of *King's Rhapsody* on the night of February 26th. He continued to play through the week, spent the weekend at Redroofs and insisted upon going back to the theatre.

A night or two later, after the performance, he returned to his flat and collapsed. Within a few hours he was dead. The date was March 5th, 1951—Ivor was fifty-eight.

'His work,' said the theatrical historian W. MacQueen Pope, 'was distinguished by his complete understanding of the theatre and the needs of the entertainment world.'

My personal four Ivor Novellos had, each, his style. The fourth—and grandest—is the style we all remember. Is it a style we shall have no need of again? I like to think the answer to that is 'No'. Styles in entertainment move, often, like a pendulum. Perhaps we haven't seen the last of the grace of Ivor. Once he set to music words that ran:

> WHY, IF THE STARS NEVER DIE,
> IS THERE EVER GOODBYE . . .?

Why, indeed?

JACK BUCHANAN
Man About Town

The 'man about town' in *Toni* at the Shaftesbury Theatre, London in 1924.

JACK BUCHANAN

YOU DARLING,
YOU DUCKY,
YOU SWEET SO AND SO,
YOU SWEET THING,
YOU NEAT THING,
YOU SET ME AGLOW!
MY FOND GIRL,
MY BLONDE GIRL,
MY SWEET THIS AND THAT,
WITHOUT YOU MY LIFE WOULD BE FLAT . . .!

A single figure, centre stage, is singing. He wears top hat and tails; he is the only Jack Buchanan. The theatre is the Lewisham Hippodrome in South East London. It isn't there any more—as the playwright put it, 'If it's beautiful and you like it, it won't be there in the morning.' That's why I'm glad I spent so many of my yesterday nights here. Not that the outside has anything of beauty, but inside the goings-on are unmatchable, life-enhancing . . .

I'VE LOTS OF OTHER WORDS FOR YOUR ATTENTION
AND ONE OR TWO I DAREN'T EVEN MENTION . . .

It is springtime 1928. *That's a Good Girl* is on its way to the London Hippodrome but I, a schoolboy, am able to give it—in the new American slang we are picking up from the talkies—'the

208

once-over' before it 'hits' the West End. I sit in the front row of
the gods and lap up every word, every note. I am at an age when I
love not one girl but all the girls, in particular the ones up there
on the screen or down there on the stage . . .

> MY VENUS
> MY GODDESS,
> LET ME BE YOUR BEAU
> AND YOU BE MY SWEET SO AND SO!

As I look about me I see the odd gaping schoolgirl. Very odd,
some of them—I wonder how I look to them . . . They, too, must
have let tonight's homework go by the board. It isn't every day a
star like Jack Buchanan comes to the local—the picture house,
yes, but here he is live on the stage. I sit here wondering, if I
grow up to be like Mr Buchanan, will the ladies fancy me as they
fancy him? The schoolgirls, no doubt, are wondering, if they
grow up fast enough, will they be in time to make a sweet so and
so for Mr Buchanan? La Ronde of the very young.

Mr Buchanan's leading lady in *That's a Good Girl* is Elsie
Randolph. We in the Gods lean forward to enjoy their duet
'Fancy our meeting' to the full. This gallery is pretty steep, in the
front row we are in some danger of toppling over and landing in
the stalls. It is Elsie Randolph's first starring part. What a pair,
what a song, what an evening, right from that first unusual
Buchanan entrance when on danced the male chorus in two rows
wearing full evening dress, their backs to the audience . . . An
immediate, excited murmur from us for we knew one of them
was Jack Buchanan. They all turned . . . and there he was; the
house roared its welcome.

The final curtain calls . . . Jack Buchanan all grace and modesty
as one lady in the gallery to my left gives Miss Randolph a
bouquet in a few called-out words 'You're wonderful, Elsie . . .'
Elsie looks up and Mr Buchanan leads her forward to take yet
another bow. *That's a Good Girl* is a palpable hit. Clutching my
autograph album I dash up the thirty or so steps to the back of

the gallery, then down another ninety-eight or so to the exit. This is in the alley-way that also has the stage door. Television hasn't been invented—or marketed: John Logie Baird is trying to get support for his idea, as is Marconi. One day, though, thankfully, we don't know it, television will bring a familiarity that will breed public contempt or, at the least, indifference. For now the magic, the mystery, is still there. A huge, expectant crowd hugs the stage door and Mr Buchanan's car. We wait for perhaps half an hour, awed, respectful. Out come other members of the cast who give their autographs. You try to get the full company . . . Kate Cutler, Raymond Newell who is making his first appearance in the musical theatre (thirty years later he will be my father-in-law in my first musical, *Chrysanthemum*) . . . Then, the hush . . . followed by a murmur growing rapidly into something like a cheer as Mr Buchanan emerges with Miss Randolph. They step into his open car. Our books are signed as they sit on the back seat, smiling, gracious . . . This is standard star behaviour and Mr Buchanan is every inch a star.

Walter John Buchanan—more simply, Jack—was the most eligible bachelor in the ladies' fantasies. The men longed to be in his highly polished shoes and know his dazzling secret. He defied ordinary analysis. He couldn't sing that well, he couldn't dance that well—he was self-taught and it showed. He was neither a great actor nor a great comedian but he was, we have to come back to it, a bright, shining star in the true theatrical meaning of a now meaningless word. When he stepped on to a stage, even with his back to us, magic had entered, and you couldn't take your eyes off him. In 1927 Madam Elinor Glyn had coined the only word that would do, a word to define the indefinable . . . Mr Buchanan had 'It'.

At the time of *That's a Good Girl* I had seen Jack in silent pictures as *Battling Butler*, as Bulldog Drummond in *The Third Round* . . . Like Ivor Novello, Buchanan, to me, was before anything else a film star. We didn't know it, of course, but he had gone through the mill. Life began well enough for him. He was born in Helensburgh, the fashionable seaside resort near Glasgow, on April 2nd, 1890. He was distantly related to Buchanan whisky. Even when young, Jack loved playing the fool, and at school they called him 'Chump'. One of his boyhood friends was John Logie Baird.

Buchanan Sr was an auctioneer but one who fancied his luck as a fancier of horses. The American wit Will Rogers thought it sad that these four-legged creatures should be the downfall of so many two-legged ones. In his view, horses are wiser than we are. 'You don't,' he said, 'catch horses betting on humans.' For Buchanan the auctioneer the hammer fell, financially. When, in time, he himself was knocked down and Mrs Buchanan took stock, the odds were not that promising. The whisky connection offered not even a small measure of help. Mrs Buchanan moved with Jack and his older sister, Jessie, to Glasgow and began taking in lodgers.

Young Jack, after a touch of failure as an auctioneer and a touch of success in amateur operatics, made a bid to be a professional comedian. It didn't bear fruit—except in that the audience threw it. His biggest laugh came when the stage manager lowered the curtain on his act and it hit him, a story he could later tell with humour. He wasn't the worst act on the bill, he claimed. The name of the Hall was Pickard's Panopticon and the audience came not so much to listen as to take aim. Jack said the little man who was on ahead of him got enough fruit thrown at him to fill a barrow. At last he began to cry and made his way to the exit. The audience quietened down at his plight and he was encouraged to turn to them before he disappeared. 'I'll tell you something,' he announced. 'Ya've missed a bloody guid song!' He went off to a huge round of applause.

As time went by, Jack would have many a bloody good song tailor-made for him. Even the reach-me-downs by Jerome Kern and such would suit. His first step, however, following that debacle, was to drop the stand-up comedy, go to London and give thought to the Buchanan image. His first break came in 1913. He understudied Vernon Watson, who later re-named himself 'Nosmo King', in a revue called *All the Winners*, and played when Mr Watson was what we describe as 'off'. He did so well that Watson was 'on' again in no time at all. Mrs Buchanan moved to London to be near Jack. She and Jessie looked after boarders in Brixton, but money was as tight as ever.

Jack was six feet tall and, because of his early privations, excessively slim. Often he lived all day on a bacon roll and a cup of tea. They turned him down for service in the First World War, leaving him wide open to being presented with white feathers. Young ladies had a way of handing these to young men who, in their view, should be at the front keeping Britain safe for them. 'We don't want to lose you but we think you ought to go' was the sinister song of the moment. Basil Hallam, an idol of Jack's who had made famous the song 'I'm Gilbert the Filbert' was also unfit for service. The white feathers he received each night at the stage door caused him to wangle his way into the Observer Corps. He was soon to die on active service. The fact that Jack never looked too healthy may have helped. Certainly it brought out the mother instinct in ladies who might otherwise have prodded him into the trenches.

He toured as an understudy to Jack Hulbert and appeared for him at a matinée in Cardiff. Ivor Novello happened to be in front. He introduced himself after the performance and suggested Jack call on George Grossmith, another Buchanan idol, when next in London. Grossmith, dapper and, like Basil Hallam, always beautifully dressed, had just made a success in *Tonight's the Night* which contained the Kern and Reynolds song 'They didn't believe me'. He cast Jack in his part for the tour, even coaching him in it. Jack was always a bundle of nerves on the stage—never, perhaps, having forgotten the night when the curtain fell on him at Pickard's Panopticon. At that time, in the school of well-tailored theatrical aristocrats it was important to have the careless air that went with the clothes. Charles Hawtrey was the famous exponent of this, and the young A. E. Matthews was learning his relaxation from him. Jack Buchanan proceeded to pick up stylish pointers from the un-beautiful but immaculate, easy Grossmith.

Tonight's the Night kept Jack playing—and working, which is the same thing for an actor—for more than a year. He was able to put a little much needed cash into the Buchanan coffers. He spent a good deal on clothes, following Grossmith's example and believing this to be professionally necessary ... but nothing on dancing lessons, the line having to be drawn somewhere. He had watched and learnt from the American soft shoe star Eugene Stratton and perhaps graceful movement was enough. It would have to be. Moreover, Jack's health would never have stood up to the strenuous training that goes to make an Astaire. I'm pretty certain he didn't watch Jack Hulbert since Hulbert, for all his charm and dry humour and his successful application of the two, was an appalling dancer. Indeed, Hulbert's footwork may have misguided Buchanan into a feeling that no advance on that would be needed. In fact, it wasn't.

Hulbert made way for Buchanan again when he was called up and had to leave the cast of the André Charlot revue *Bubbly*. Revue followed revue now until, in 1921, Jack co-stared with Gertrude Lawrence in Charlot's *A to Z*. In this, he sang, 'And her mother came too', which had words by Dion Titheradge and a melody by Ivor Novello. In 1922 he went into management, presenting and starring in *Battling Butler*. He charmed American audiences in André Charlot's *1924 Revue*, with Gertrude Lawrence and Beatrice Lillie, and again in Charlot's *1926 Revue*. He had entered silent films as early as 1919 but it was 1925 before I saw him as Bulldog Drummond in *The Third Round*. I have the movie at home. It isn't very good, distance lending disenchantment. On the other hand, absolutely nothing is lost when I hear the sounds that were made so long ago. In singing Jack showed no favouritism when it came to a choice between one octave and another. In 'Goodnight Vienna' he switches up and down disgracefully but at every playing the magic comes at you straight out of the speaker.

The twenties and thirties were Jack Buchanan's golden years. They were the golden years for everyone, rich and poor alike, who had the guts to eschew self-pity and knew how to dream. No

matter how dreary your day, how low your hopes, you could visit
the local flicks for what we called 'six penn'orth of dark'. If you
could plonk down ninepence for what were known as 'late doors'
and had your health and strength you could climb all the way up
to the gods at the local theatre and dwell for nearly three hours in
cloud-cuckoo land. It is a pejorative term, but there was great joy
in being a tenant there. The impresarios saw to it that you were in
the lap of luxury. The musical comedies invited you to country
house parties with maids galore, lady guests who were certain to
strip for swimming and male guests who arrived wearing plus-
fours or white flannels and the famous footwear that was white
with brown leather toe-caps—co-respondent shoes, by generally
agreed name. The males were usually stony broke, to make you
feel at home. Once under that gloriously unreal roof you could
put out of mind the landlord who owned yours and whose rent
was forever due . . .

The big Buchanan event of 1926 was his appearance, under his
own management, in *Sunny* at the London Hippodrome. Kern,
Harbach and Hammerstein had created it. *Sunny* had been a
smash hit on Broadway, and was as big a hit now for Buchanan in
London. His co-star was Binnie Hale. Also in the cast of *Sunny*
was Miss Elsie Randolph who, when Jack presented *That's a
Good Girl* two years later, moved into the star position. Jack as an
actor-manager was not an employer in the usual theatrical mould.
According to Elsie:

> 'We were just like a family. It broke our hearts when the plays
> came off—although we knew there was going to be another
> one. We were together all the time. We'd play golf in the
> mornings, have a snooze in the afternoon, meet again at the
> theatre . . . He'd knock on the door and say "All right, dear?"
> I'd say, "Yes, thank you." We'd chat . . . We never went on
> the stage cold . . .'

This was the kind of togetherness young actors in the important
companies try to achieve today by meeting for warm-ups before

the performances. Play hard, work hard—the head of this happy
family continued to film in Britain and in Hollywood. He made
Paris with Irene Bordoni, the star who had come to Broadway
from Corsica, and *Monte Carlo* with Jeannette MacDonald under
the direction of Ernst Lubitsch. On Broadway, he joined Jessie
Matthews in Cochran's *Wake Up and Dream* . . . Jack had entered
what was to be the last decade before the pirates moved in.
Innocence was walking the plank but we had yet to feel the sword
prodding us in the backside.

1931 gave us *Stand Up and Sing*, a typical title of the day. It
had an untypical title song with new rhythms. Jack was part-
author, with Douglas Furber. Stage success, screen success . . .
the joy was dispensed to the public and the money rolled in, in
payment. Furber recalled the ease with which it rolled out again
from Jack's ever-open pocket. Duggie had written many librettos
for Jack and the words for dozens of his songs; he was lyrical
about the over-generosity:

'Money meant nothing to him. His tips to waiters, car drivers
and stage door cadgers were in the millionaire class. I once
asked him the reason for such munificence. "I've known what
it means to be poor," he answered. Jack was a gambler. A very
unusual one because he seldom backed a horse or played a
card. He went in for big business. The bigger the business, the
more money he lost. One morning he rang up to tell me he'd
discovered a genius—an old schoolfellow from Scotland. I
must meet him, all his friends must meet him, he was
arranging a lunch. A day or two later he brought us into
contact with a wild-eyed, shaggy-looking Scot whom he
presented to us as "Mr John Logie Baird". Baird had
discovered television. Jack decided to finance him. He in-
vested every penny he could spare and he dragged his friends
in too but we lost every penny we put in. Baird was a genius all
right but a little ahead of his time. After this Jack lay low for a
while—so low that I guessed there was something in the offing.
Then the bubble burst. He would build for himself a big and

beautiful theatre in the very heart of theatreland. He achieved
his ambition. He built the Leicester Square Theatre. It cost
him a fortune . . .'

In 1933 Jack made the movie *Yes, Mr Brown*, co-directing too,
with Herbert Wilcox. The following year he undertook solo the
direction of *That's a Good Girl*. In February of 1935 he was back
at the Hippodrome in *Mr Whittington*, with Elsie Randolph as his
co-star. It was a fine score, this time with music by the American
Johnny Green, whose biggest hits had been 'Body and soul' and
'I cover the waterfront'. Duggie Furber shared the lyrical
honours with Greatrex Newman. Together the trio produced
'Weep no more' and 'Oceans of time' for *Mr Whittington*. In
September 1937 *This'll Make You Whistle* opened at the Palace
Theatre, London, with the same style, the same innocence . . .
and the same leading lady.

The greatest limiting factor of all, of course, is time. For the
Jack Buchanan school of charm theatre, and for his films, it was
running out. Noël Coward, ten years his junior, would begin to
lose steam some ten years later—it seems to have been a matter of
simple mathematics. Perhaps we could give Noël fifteen years
before the repeats began. For an actor there are no repeats of his
stage performances, which are painted on the memory alone.
Wherever people reminisce the performances may spring
momentarily to life, but there is no forever canvas, no published
music, no printed page. Buchanan was fast becoming a beautiful
anachronism. The sounds he put on records are, as I have said, a
different story. They are evocative almost to a point where the
original magic is, if not to be captured again, to be sensed deeply.

Jack's poor luck in the gambling field gave way to better in the
Second World War—or it could be seen that way. He told this
story at the height of the blitz:

'A few years ago I was responsible for building a theatre in the
West End of London and while I was about it I thought it
would be a good idea to build a duplex apartment on top of the

theatre for myself to live in. So I've been living there for ... I suppose seven or eight years. All was well until a week or ten days ago. I happened not to be there one night and on that particular night our friends from the other side of the North Sea took it into their heads to drop a nice heavy one right there and I'm afraid my flat and office and everything's gone. I was out with some people who wanted to hit the high spots, have a laugh or two. I wanted to get home early as a matter of fact because I had to work first thing in the morning. They persuaded me to stay and I was a bit late getting home ... a very good thing for me, believe me!'

In 1948 Jack appeared in New York in *Harvey* and, later the same year, in *Don't Listen Ladies* which he also co-presented with Lee Ephraim. He brought the play to the St James's Theatre London in January of 1949. He also brought over a wife. He had married Mrs Susan Bassett, to the astonishment of the press, his friends and, most of all, of the lady who had been his accepted constant companion.

His New York visit led to his co-starring with Fred Astaire in MGM's *The Band Wagon* in 1953. The success of the film introduced Jack to a whole new generation of admirers. His song and dance duet with Fred to the Schwartz and Dietz classic 'I guess I'll have to change my plan' is a rich legacy to us all. The dance was soft shoe—a wise choice, as Buchanan wouldn't have stood an earthly tapping with Astaire. But even Astaire couldn't outdo him in grace of movement, it was an interesting match. Interesting too, sadly so, was the fact that the character Jack played so well was that of a star passing his prime ... an anachronism.

Jack Buchanan returned to a Britain about to be swamped by the grandly misnamed 'New Wave'. He appeared at the Garrick Theatre in a trashy comedy called *As Long As They're Happy*. It was about appeasement, not the appeasement that had been Neville Chamberlain's forte, but the New Appeasement, the appeasement of children by parents. I saw the play and thought that, good as he was, Jack was miles out of his element in a piece about pop singing. On impulse, I called in afterwards at the stage door. I had never met him. Nearly thirty years had passed since I collected his autograph but time has a way of meaning very little to me, except in that it carries a scythe. I was invited at once to his dressing room. He appeared to know all about me and made me quite at home. When I mentioned that I had written a song I would like him to consider singing, he said something nice about my writing, and suggested I come to his flat in Mount Street the following day, which I did. I met his attractive American wife and again was made very much at home. I played and sang the song, called 'If I could take my pick I'd pick Piccadilly', and he said he'd love to sing it. He was about to begin a series of broadcasts for the B.B.C. under the title *Man About Town* and would include it in one of the programmes if it was all right with me. I thought back to the night at the Lewisham Hippodrome stage door when he had signed my book. I didn't tell him about that, thinking, perhaps, that he wouldn't care for it very much but . . . would I mind if Jack Buchanan sang one of my songs . . .? His photograph graces the published copy today.

Then I remembered a song I had written during wartime called 'Man About Town'. I played it and sang it, and had barely lifted my fingers from the keyboard of his piano when Jack said: 'That's going to be my theme song, old boy.' Then he went on: 'How would you like to be in the series? Appear as yourself . . . write songs for me . . .?' It was all agreed in no time. We worked out an idea. It would be announced that I would write a new London song each week for the 'Man About Town' to sing. I had one or two already in the drawer but I did, in fact, write some half a dozen songs specifically for the series. The broadcasts took place on the Garrick Theatre stage, with an audience.

Jack was not too much in evidence at rehearsals. His office was only upstairs and we supposed he was deep in big business. On one occasion the full company kicked its heels in the auditorium for two hours, waiting for him. Beautiful, serene Adele Dixon looked as cool at the end of it as when she had walked in bang on

The published copy of the first song I ever sang to Jack – and the first of mine sung by him. The picture is the one that still hangs in the bar of the Garrick Theatre.

time, but others were about to get ruffled. Suddenly, down the
aisle came Jack, unflurried, immaculate . . . wearing, as he always
did, his trilby hat. The only times I saw him without that hat
were in Mount Street and in the flat he rented in Brighton. I
don't know why he wore it indoors when working: Crosby wore
one because he had no hair but Jack had plenty. Does a hat give
you confidence? Did he need it? Had it something to do with
Pickard's Panopticon—keeping yourself ready for a getaway?
Jack murmured a deep word of apology and the assembly was at
his feet.

This difficulty about getting Jack to rehearse led to worry. A
new song every week . . . songs need to be studied and learnt.
The Bill Shepherd Chorus was in support and Bill did the vocal
arrangements, decided where the chorus should come in, which
bits Jack should sing solo. One week I produced a particularly
tricky song. 'He'll never get it in the time,' said Bill. The matter
was resolved by giving Jack the minimum of solo and the chorus
the maximum of back-up. Jack arrived in his own not too good
time, did his usual warm-up of the company with his charm, and
then picked up his song copy. 'Now we're for it,' Bill Shepherd
whispered to me, 'I think I've only given him about eight bars
solo . . .' We looked at Jack who was glancing at the music. 'Ah
well,' he said at last . . . 'I see you've rumbled me.'

Jack opted to sing several of my songs in cabaret at the Café de
Paris. Gilbert Brown, his personal manager, broached the matter
of terms. I'm not going to haggle, I thought. Not over this, not
with Jack. It did occur to me to ask Gilbert Brown to make a
suggestion but I didn't want him to suggest too little. I couldn't
imagine what reply I would have made if he had. It was like those
bridge things in a fairground that shake you to pieces—I didn't
want to step on to it. I said, 'I don't want anything, Mr Brown.
Just a table for two and supper with champagne and no bill.'
That's how I was able to enjoy Jack's first night in cabaret to the
full.

Before the cabaret I went into Jack's dressing room to wish
him luck, and I've never in my life seen a performer more

nervous. He wasn't completely at home with some of the new material. I had reminded him that Noël Coward had used old and tried material only in his cabaret appearance, and of course, had also written the songs himself, which gave him a bonus of calm. There was a certain amount of fluffing here and there but, in the main, the evening went well. When Jack came out with a medley of his known hits he brought the Café down.

Gilbert Brown spoke with great affection of the morning routine at the theatre with his boss:

'My office at the Garrick was on the opposite side of the corridor to his. When he was in London—he spent a good deal of time abroad, principally in America—he would arrive at the office during the morning, go straight to his room, do a *lot* of telephoning . . . and if there was nothing urgent about which he wanted to see me I wouldn't hear anything from him until about one o'clock when he would open his door . . . and, in the accent of the Southern states, call out, "Massa Brown . . . hows about a li'l' snort?" I'd call, "Massa Buchan' . . . that's a swell notion, try holdin' me back!" Then, into his room . . . and, over a gin and tonic, we would discuss his plans, problems and what have you for about an hour. Then, to lunch . . .'

One morning Jack telephoned me to ask why I didn't look in at the Garrick Theatre for a glass of something. I couldn't think of a reason—I didn't try hard. It was a casual invitation but it had a touch of urgency. I don't know why I thought so but, to this day, I do. There he was, sitting at his desk, immaculate from pearl-grey trilby to highly polished shoes. I had met Green, his faithful dresser-cum-valet, and wouldn't have expected anything else. We chatted, we sipped . . . we chatted. Jack seemed unable to get to the point, if point indeed there was. We sipped . . . gin and tonic . . . We talked about the pirates whose grappling irons had made scratches on our sleek craft—the year was 1956. We talked of the world as it spun before the falling of graciousness from grace. We took the present-day world apart and couldn't put it together again, the trouble everyone would be having ... We sipped ... we talked of the New Wave that was dirtying up our nice, clean beach and wondered, should we lie down and let it wash over us like Noël Coward in that film *The Scoundrel*... or should we stand up and sing, get with it? I reminded Jack of something Noël had said. 'Don't try too hard to be with it, you may end up by being without it.' Jack opened another bottle and we sipped again. 'While supplies last,' he said ... The gin was excellent. The tonic might have been excellent too, for all we knew. Finally, after a two-hour session of absolutely nothing but delight, I left him. I carried with me the strong but surely quite ludicrous feeling that Jack Buchanan needed a friend...

He died some eighteen months later, on October 21st, 1957, after a long and painful illness. He was a shy man, easily embarrassed when he was among members of the public who recognized him. The end, for Jack, came in a London hospital—in a public ward. Duggie Furber spoke a few simple truths in tribute...

'On the day after he left us I read in one of our leading newspapers that he was one of the richest men in the theatre. Others tried to make me hazard a guess at his fortune. I didn't answer them because I sensed he would leave next to nothing. He earned the best part of a million during his long and colourful career...'

In today's terms, ten times as much...

'... but he had many pensioners and he never refused a loan. If only half the people who owed him money had repaid him this might be a very different story...'

Duggie summed him up at last in these words...

'Dear Jack ... So quiet, so modest, so generous ... He spread a lot of happiness and he never behaved like a star...'

Duggie meant by that that he was never temperamental nor rude but this is behaviour you get from pretenders only. And Jack was no pretender to stardom.

Tributes came from all over the world, from leaders of the theatre and cinema who had shared stage and screen with him ... political leaders and leaders among those whose part it is to criticize. Richard Watts wrote in the *New York Post:*

'In a time when all sorts of performers are loosely called "great", Jack Buchanan was one who really deserved the title.'

Again, I hark back to that first night of *That's a Good Girl*. In the words of the song, I say—not without a touch of pride because this man who was my schoolboy idol did become my friend—fancy our meeting...